The Honorable Shirley Chisholm

Congresswoman from Brooklyn

The Honorable

Shirley Chisholm

Congresswoman from Brooklyn

Nancy Hicks

Lion Books · New York · 1971

To my wonderful little David

CONTENTS

The Honorable Shirley Chisholm

Congresswoman from Brooklyn

Chapter 1

Unbossed and Unbought

She stands about five feet tall and is skinny. Very skinny. Her legs are thin and shaped like bows. Her eyes are very dark, almost black, and they shine with a little twinkle when the light catches them. Most of the time they are covered with black-framed eyeglasses that taper into neat little points. She is attractive without being pretty, and she is always immaculately groomed. She usually wears a dress with a matching jacket and color-coordinated shoes and handbag.

To look at her you might think she is a nice librarian. Not frail, although her size can give that impression, but certainly easy-going. Do not be fooled! This lady is tough. If she happens to speak before you finish forming an opinion of her, then you won't make any mistake. Her mouth is her political weapon, and she is not afraid to use it.

She is Congresswoman Shirley A. Chisholm, member of the House of Representatives from New York's

Twelfth °Congressional District in Brooklyn, the first
black woman ever elected to the Congress of the
United States.

She's tough and uncompromising, the champion of
unpopular causes. She is hated by professional politicians but loved by those who vote for her. She is, in
short, a people's politician.

Before her election to the Ninety-first Congress on
November 5, 1968, this 98-pound political heavyweight
was a schoolteacher, a relatively unknown soldier in
the ranks of the Democratic party of Brooklyn. By
August, 1971, she was so well known that she could de-
clare herself a candidate for president. She has always
had a reputation for being a maverick—a person who
knows his or her mind and follows it, whether it is safe
to do so or not.

"I am unbossed and unbought," she says over and
over again. "This is my symbol, and I intend to maintain it even if it costs me my political life. I rose to
prominence because of my ability to take a stand. If
I change now, the young and black people in this
country would be disillusioned. If you are a leader,
you're supposed to act like one. You're not supposed
to straddle. I want to be this kind of free agent until
I die."

This is the story of the life of this free agent—
from Brooklyn to Barbados and back to Brooklyn, from
teaching to her entry into politics and her rocket-fast
rise once she decided to take on organized government.
But behind Shirley Chisholm's story is the story of
black people in this country.

Today, we are getting used to seeing Negroes in

high offices of government. The number is growing
yearly. With the election of 1970, thirteen of the 535
seats in Congress were held by blacks. But until one
hundred years ago, black people in America were not
considered whole human beings—much less able to
hold office or even vote. During the days of slavery a
black was counted, according to the Constitution of
the United States, as three-fifths of a person. This was
a compromise, because there were some at the Con-
stitutional Convention who didn't want to count blacks
at all. The reason why the question was serious is that
the number of members a state has in the House of
Representatives depends on population. If the South
could count slaves, even at a discount, it would have
gained more congressmen.

Change came with the end of the Civil War and the
period called Reconstruction. Besides freeing slaves
from the bondage of the plantation, Congress gave the
black man citizenship by the Civil Rights Act of 1866.
This act was supposed to guarantee equality in housing
and employment and set the tone for a more sympa-
thetic attitude on the part of white Americans toward
black. But these federal laws were trampled on. Individual states passed laws that became known as the
"black codes." Under these, unemployed Negroes could
be fined and jailed as vagrants, and all blacks were
prevented from socializing with white people by legally
segregated public facilities.

The Republican party, the party of Abraham Lincoln,
controlled Congress at that time, and didn't agree with
what the states were doing.

In 1865, Congress set up the Freedmen's Bureau,

which gave ex-slaves basic health and education services. Then, in 1867, it passed the First Reconstruction
Act, which gave Negroes the right to vote. By 1870,
the Fourteenth and Fifteenth Amendments to the Constitution had further broadened the rights of black
people.

Voter-registration drives began. By 1867, qualified
black voters in the South outnumbered white voters by
almost forty-five thousand. Blacks were in the majority
in South Carolina, Alabama, Louisiana, Mississippi, and
Florida. In some of those states, black voters outnumbered whites by almost two to one.

Negroes began to appear at all levels of government.
There were black state legislators and city councilmen
and school-board representatives. Between 1870 and
1902, twenty-two blacks served in the Congress—two
of them as senators.

Their political reputations varied. Many were considered ineffective "tokens," manipulated by white politicians. Others were critized for not really caring about
the future of black people. But most of the black congressmen fought for the equality of black people in
America.

Whatever their motives, they were not around long
enough to accomplish very much. By 1902 there was not
one black left in Congress. In fact, by that time there
was not even a single black legislator anywhere in the
country. One of the tactics that created this situation
was gerrymandering. Gerrymandering involves redrawing the lines of voter districts with no other purpose
than to give one group an advantage over another.

Many districts with black majorities were split up to form parts of districts with white majorities. The black man in America had lost his right to help elect officials of government.

Not until 1929 was another Negro elected to Congress. He was Oscar DePriest of Chicago, the first black man elected in the twentieth century and the last Negro Republican to receive the backing of a predominantly black electorate. DePriest's election—and that of other blacks after him—was the result of a national population shift. In the early 1900's many black people left poor southern farmlands in the hopes of doing better in the large cities of the North.

In the presidential election year of 1932, most black people switched their party from Republican, the party of Lincoln, to Democratic, the party of Franklin D. Roosevelt. These were Depression years, and the blacks suffering in the cities were desperate for change. President Roosevelt started the New Deal program, which provided jobs and housing and welfare for the poor. In America, that has always included the majority of black people.

Over the years, a few more black congressmen were elected. The most influential and controversial was the Reverend Adam Clayton Powell, Jr., from the Eighteenth Congressional District in New York. That's Harlem—the country's largest black community.

He served more than twenty years in Congress, some of that time as chairman of the influential Education and Labor Committee. He fought against segregation on military bases around the world and against segre-

gated public facilities in the South and North. He spon-
sored laws providing federal aid to education and a
minimum federal wage.

Yet Adam Clayton Powell, like Shirley Chisholm after
him, was not at all popular in Congress. Besides his
outspoken stance, he was considered by many to be a
playboy, despite his position as pastor of the Abyssinian
Baptist Church, with its huge congregation.

Finally, in 1967, Adam Clayton Powell's congressional
colleagues took official action against him in a vote of
censure. They charged that he had refused to pay the
fine and damages in a defamation-of-character suit that
he had lost against a Harlem woman; that he had mis-
used travel funds; and that he kept his wife on the
payroll of his Washington staff when she actually lived
most of the year in Puerto Rico. The House of Representatives fined him, withdrew his pay, stripped him of his
seniority, and refused to let him take his seat. He took
his case to court and went into a self-imposed exile on
the Caribbean island of Bimini. While the case was
pending, the people of Harlem re-elected him to Congress even though he was not in the country. The House
still refused to seat him.

Many black people, including Shirley Chisholm, were
angered by this action. A white senator from Connec-
ticut, Thomas A. Dodd, had also been censured, for
misusing campaign funds. But he was neither fined nor
denied his seat. Black people felt that because Powell
had refused to apologize, as he was asked to do, white
congressmen were punishing him for his independence.
The courts finally ruled that Powell should be given
back his seat. He refused to take it, holding out for his

back pay and seniority. Seniority is important in Congress because those who have served longest get preference for the important committees and committee chairmanships.

Powell had spent so much time in exile that other political forces in Harlem began working for his seat. Even those black people who initially supported him believed that he should have returned to Congress immediately after the court ruled in his favor. They felt that the people of Harlem had gone unrepresented long enough. As a result, Powell lost the 1970 Democratic party primary for the seat he had held for twenty-five years to a young black lawyer, Charles Rangel.

Despite those who speak against him—black and white—the story of Adam Clayton Powell has had special meaning for black people. To many, he was a black man who took a stand, who spoke out, and then was politically assassinated.

The courts, which proved to be a friend to Powell, gave Shirley Chisholm her start in national politics. In 1968, while she was serving her third term as a New York State assemblywoman from Brooklyn, the courts ruled on the district lines in Brooklyn. The decision dealt with representation—how many people should vote for one elected official. It led to the creation of a new congressional district, which would include much of the largely black Bedford-Stuyvesant section. The election of Brooklyn's first black representative was assured.

Brooklyn is very important to Shirley Chisholm's story. It is one of New York City's five boroughs. The others are Manhattan, the main business area, and the

Bronx, Queens, and Staten Island. Of all the eight million people who live in the city, more live in Brooklyn than in any other borough.

The borough may be best known as the home of the Brooklyn Dodgers baseball team, which left New York for Los Angeles in the 1950's. Now most non-New Yorkers probably think of Brooklyn as Coney Island, with its beach and amusement park and Nathan's hot dogs.

But when it comes right down to it, Brooklyn is just another place—larger than most—where many different kinds of people live. At the beginning of the century, it was a region of farms, which gave way to private homes. At one time, it had a thriving business district. It has many neighborhoods that housed immigrants from Europe. Jews settled in the tenements of Brownsville and later in the one-family houses of Flatbush. Italians settled all the way out near the Atlantic Ocean in an area known as Gravesend.

Intellectuals and writers made their homes in the narrow brownstones of Brooklyn Heights, the closest area to Manhattan. The wealthy lived in huge mansions along broad, tree-shaded boulevards like Ocean Parkway in the middle of the borough.

In the 1920's and 30's, southern blacks who came North went to Chicago or to Harlem, but West Indian immigrants from the islands of the Caribbean—like Shirley Chisholm's family—settled in Brooklyn.

Today, most of Brooklyn's middle-class population has moved eastward to Long Island. Bedford-Stuyvesant, the largest and most stable black community in the borough, suffers terrible economic problems. Much of its housing is substandard. There are few jobs. The public schools are far from being what the parents would like them to be. Nor are health services what they should be.

These problems are even worse in other communities. Brownsville, once a predominantly Jewish residential community, looks today like a bombed-out area left over from World War II. There are buildings only half-standing with bricks crumbling from the walls. The streets are covered with garbage and abandoned cars. What used to be businesses housed in storefronts along Dean Street and Hopkinson Avenue are now just hollow shells in the ground floors of abandoned buildings. They remind the poor residents, mostly black and Puerto Rican, that this was once a lively and prosperous community.

The people of Brooklyn look at all of this, and they wonder why. Certainly, they are poor and have no economic power, but they do have the power of the vote. For years they have been responsible for electing men to serve in the state government or in Congress, men supposedly fighting for their rights and for a better life for them. But what has happened? What were these men doing for them?

With the rising black awareness of the 1960's, a new idea spread among the country's largest minority group. Black community organizers said: "We cannot really expect white people to care what happens to us. We will have to find and develop our own leaders to fight for us." They did.

One of the first, most fierce, and now most famous was Shirley Chisholm.

"I am a historical person at this point, and I am very

much aware of it," she says of her position in national politics. "There is in this country a vacuum of leadership that people really feel they can trust. This is especially true since the deaths of Martin Luther King and Senator Robert Kennedy.

"I'm not great. It's just that I don't operate on political expediency. I'm not a hypocrite and I don't doubletalk. The people are sick of listening to mealy-mouthed election phrases. They like politicians who have the courage to tell them the truth.

"The people are looking for politicians with integrity. Until there is another loud, black voice, I seem to be filling some of that vacuum."

Chapter 2

Early Years

In the early 1920's, when Brooklyn was still a place that inspired hope, two young people arrived there by separate boats from the West Indian island of Barbados. The man had been a factory shoemaker, the woman a skilled seamstress. They were looking for that indefinable "good life" that most immigrants seek. He was easy-going and good-natured, tall and handsome with a head of fluffy hair that would later turn white and glisten in the sun. She was small and reserved, quiet and religious. They were Charles St. Hill and Ruby Seale.

Charles St. Hill had been born in British Guiana (now called Guyana) and spent a part of his life in Cuba before moving to Barbados. Ruby was from Barbados. In Brooklyn they found each other and married. They settled in an apartment on Jefferson Avenue in the predominantly Jewish Brownsville section, and they awaited the birth of their first child.

The good life they had hoped for was terribly slow in coming. Charles St. Hill found a job as an unskilled laborer in a burlap factory, and Ruby worked at home as a seamstress. When things got very bad, she worked as a domestic.

Then, on a brisk fall morning, November 30, 1924, the first of their four daughters was born. The couple named her Shirley Anita. From the very beginning, there was something special about the child. She began walking and talking before most children do. She was assertive. Even at an extremely early age, she seemed to have the makings of a leader.

Her father adored her. He called her "Shirls," and she called him "Pop." Their closeness was resented by her younger sisters, Odessa, Muriel, and Selma, and in time led to a family split.

Back in those days when the children were young, times were bad. But the family was hopeful, and Charles St. Hill worked hard. In three consecutive years, his wife presented him with his first three daughters. They grew and thrived.

But the life that was to bring the St. Hills prosperity and leisure just never materialized. The girls were getting older and more money was needed to care for them. And what of their education? The parents, despite their differing outlooks on the world, wanted a good education for all their daughters, and a laborer's job in a burlap factory did not seem enough to do it. So, like many young West Indian parents in this country, they decided to send their children back to the islands to be raised and educated by grandparents. The St. Hills would continue to work in New York, living a marginal

existence, sending money to the islands, and storing
every spare penny in savings for the future of their
daughters.

The day for departure arrived. The morning was
hectic as Ruby St. Hill packed everything and dressed
Shirley, Odessa, and Muriel, while Charles paced, constantly checking the clock and warning his wife that
she'd better hurry or she would miss the boat. She was
always missing things—church, meetings, appoint-
ments, family gatherings. Ruby was always late. So
this morning was especially anxious for Charles St. Hill.
He did not want his daughters to leave, but he could
not stand a second morning of readying them for the
trip.

Finally, Ruby St. Hill with her three daughters, aged
four, three, and two, rushed out of the house and down
to the dock, from which the ship was to sail. But they
were too late. Ruby St. Hill timidly returned home.

Her husband's anger was short-lived. The very next
day, November 14, 1928, the boat that the girls had
been scheduled to take, the *Vestris,* sank off the Vir-
ginia coast with more than one hundred persons lost.
Ruby St. Hill's habit of lateness had saved her children's
lives.

Within the week, mother and daughters were on
another ship on their way to Barbados. As soon as they
landed, they headed for Bridgetown, the island's largest
city, and from there to the lush farm nine miles away
that belonged to Fitz Herbert Seale and his wife,
Emmeline, the children's grandparents.

Shirley quickly settled into life on the spacious farm,
where she played with the animals and helped with the

gardening and small chores. There was a lot of land, and plenty of room and adult supervision for the nine children who lived there.

Besides Shirley and her sisters there were six of her cousins. Ruby's unmarried sister, Myrtle Seale, helped teach the children the discipline of the Barbadian culture and the cleanliness that is so much a part of it.

They attended the British-run schools to learn reading and writing. The family taught them religion, studiousness, and stick-to-itiveness.

Shirley was growing and progressing. She was reading before her fourth birthday, and began to write not long after that. She was bright and tough—loved by the adults and respected by the other children. They had to listen to her. If they did not, Shirley, who was then a fat little girl, would beat them up.

She developed a close relationship with her grandmother, who was not a big woman but seemed that way to the children. Emmeline Seale was very stern but also very kind, and she had a great capacity to love all her grandchildren. Her gentleness made her seem like a mythical godmother to the children, and they listened closely when she would gather them around her to talk about life.

One day, when she and Shirley were alone on the farmhouse porch, she picked the little girl up and sat her on her lap and told her about success. It was a speech that Shirley would hear over and over again during the six years she lived with her mother's parents.

"Shirley, nothing can stop you if you are determined not to be distracted by the world of temptation," her grandmother said. "If you have strong character and

determination and if you apply yourself, you will rise to
the top."

Shirley began to apply that lesson with her sisters and
cousins. She was always active in sports, always competitive, and she usually won. If there was any question
about it, it meant a fight. She was forceful and outspoken and demanded that things be done her way or
not at all. She almost always got what she wanted.

But this did not make her spoiled or soft. She was
resourceful and self-sufficient. Even as a little girl she
showed signs of independence. She washed her own
socks and took care of her own possessions. And when
it came to the principle of a thing, if she thought she
was right, she would argue to the end.

It was this spirit and her superior academic work that
endeared her to the teachers at the Vauxhall Coeduca-
tional School. She went to class every day in freshly
laundered clothes, most of them made by her mother
but cared for by her aunt and grandmother. When her
teacher announced that there would be a savings plan
in the classroom, Shirley signed up and never missed
a chance to save her money.

Each week she would bring a penny or whatever the
family could afford and deposit it in the large piggy
bank that sat on the windowsill of the classroom. She
would then stand in line with her thrifty classmates,
while the teacher stamped the bankbook to register
the deposit. This went on for years. The bankbook is
still among the Seale family's possessions.

Every Sunday, the family would walk to the Vauxhall Methodist Church, where the children attended
Sunday school. Shirley loved to listen to Bible stories,

and she developed the strong religious feelings she still has today.

But her young mind was so active that she often had many thoughts going on in it at the same time, even when she was thinking of God. One night she got on her knees, as she did every night to say the Lord's Prayer. When she came to the line, "For Thine is the kingdom, and the power, and the glory," she said instead, "For Thine is the kingdom, and the power, and the suitcase."

"The suitcase?" her Aunt Myrtle asked in astonishment. "Shirley, what is that you are saying?"

"Oh, Aunt Myrt, I forgot. I was thinking of something else," she admitted.

By all measures, Shirley was thriving in the West Indies, but back in New York, Charles and Ruby St. Hill, now the parents of a fourth daughter, Selma, could no longer bear having their family separated. Charles St. Hill sent for his daughters.

On May 10, 1934, at the age of ten, Shirley left the islands to return to a Brooklyn that would not only become her home, but would also become her cause.

Charles St. Hill embraced his returning daughters. He had missed them terribly. Life was not going to be easy for the family, but he felt certain that if they were together, they would make it.

His girls were all he had hoped they would be. They were healthy and well adjusted. Most of all, they were well educated. "I like so much the way the girls were trained," he wrote to his mother-in-law. "They are bright and mannerly. I am very happy with the way they have been raised, but I had to bring them home.

I missed them. I just couldn't see my house without them."

In Brownsville, Shirley was enrolled in the third grade at Public School 144. In the West Indies, she had been in the sixth grade. But because she had missed the American curriculum in history and geography, she had to go into the lower grade.

"Mother, I'm bored," she would say when she came home from school. The third grade had nothing to teach her, and it failed to stimulate her active mind. Restless, bored, she was classified as a discipline problem. Eventually, the school faculty realized what was wrong and skipped her one grade, then two, and gave her a tutor to allow her to catch up in history and geography. Now happy in school, she gave her teachers no further trouble. Her mother worried about her school difficulties at first, but her father saw her strong will as an asset. They both knew Shirley would do something special.

At this time, the Great Depression that the country suffered through all during the 1930's was at its worst. The family's meager funds seemed to shrink even more. Ruby St. Hill went to work as a domestic in the homes of wealthy Jewish families in Flatbush. Worried about her children, she took aside Shirley, the oldest and most responsible. Ruby St. Hill placed the house key around her daughter's neck and said:

"Now, Shirley, I want you to take care of your younger sisters while Daddy and I are at work. You will be responsible for seeing that they get to school and home again, and that they get lunch. Okay?"

Shirley took to the responsibility of being a latch-key child with no trouble. Each lunchtime she would collect her sisters, bring them home, and feed them. Then she would take them back to school, attend class herself, and collect them again at three o'clock to see that they got home.

Once a week, she would take a trip to a local bakery, where she could buy a pile of leftover buns for a quarter. These would make an afternoon snack for the girls three days a week.

The family was poor, but it managed.

Ruby St. Hill remained a handy seamstress, and when she could find an extra bolt of material, she would whip up dresses for her girls. Sometimes the families she worked for would give her clothing. Her daughters looked forward to the days when their mother would arrive at the front door with a large package under her arm.

"What is it?" the girls would ask as they danced around her. "A dress? A hat? A coat?"

For about nine years the family lived this way, with both mother and father working and Shirley caring for the younger girls.

"Many people have said I don't deserve the vote of poor people because I am middle class," Shirley Chisholm says today. "They see that I dress well and speak well, and I can't blame them. They really don't know my background. They think I was born—not with a silver spoon in my mouth but maybe with a brass one. They don't know that we were poor at one time."

During these years, too, Shirley was learning about the world around her in Brownsville and about herself. With her sisters she was assertive, but she was shy with people she did not know. She made friends slowly, but once she did, she was the leader. This was the case with white and black children alike.

The West Indies that Shirley had known was a black culture, where there were no problems of racial difference. Black people managed their own affairs, business and government, and knew no other way of life. But Brownsville at this time was still mostly white. The St. Hill girls adapted to this new situation, making friends with the other children, going to their houses to do homework, inviting them to their simple apartment.

The difference in cultures fascinated Shirley and her sisters. From the window of their Brownsville apartment, they could see into the window of a synagogue that was right next door. Each Saturday morning, the Jewish sabbath, people from the neighborhood would flock to the house of worship. The men would put on their skullcaps and rock back and forth, chanting prayers. For the St. Hill girls, Saturday was not a day of rest, but a day of work. They were supposed to be cleaning the house—dusting the furniture, washing down the bathroom and kitchen, making sure that their crowded room was clean and neat. But instead, they liked to sneak out onto the fire escape and peek into the temple windows. At first, they would laugh at what they saw because it looked funny to them. Finally someone explained to them that each religion has its own practices but that all are equally expressions of devotion. After that, they would continue to go out on the fire escape, not to laugh, but just to watch. On many Saturday mornings, Ruby St. Hill would wonder why her daughters were so quiet at their household chores.

She would find them just where she expected to find them, on the fire escape. Their curiosity cost the girls many a spanking for loafing on the job.

While Shirley was still in elementary school, her family moved out of Brownsville to 420 Ralph Avenue in the Bedford-Stuyvesant section. It was the first of many moves the family would make around Brooklyn during Shirley's childhood. They were always looking for someplace better than what they had, even the slightest bit better. Charles St. Hill kept hoping to find a place big enough to allow his daughters to have two bedrooms. There was always a bedrom for the parents and another for the girls, but the St. Hills wanted their children to have a little more room, and kept moving to find it, although they never did. Finding better living quarters was an obsession with Ruby St. Hill.

Moving was never a big production. There were six people involved, but there were no elaborate furnishings. Furnishing a home for a poor family is a simple art. Trying to figure out what to buy and where to put it is hardly a problem. Almost everything is determined by need. If a lamp breaks, you fix it or buy a new one. There are no summer and winter draperies. In winter, you find the heaviest material possible to block the draft from the wind that comes through the cracks in the windows. In the summer, you strip the windows to allow the slightest breeze to make its way into the house. When a couch or chair gets too worn or dirty, you cover it, usually with a throw cloth. When the cover wears, you replace that.

Bedford-Stuyvesant brought Shirley a better home and a new awareness. In Bedford-Stuyvesant she heard

the words *black* and *nigger* for the first time. She became aware of the frustrations and hostilities of black
people, who made up the entire population of the area,
but who depended on white society to feed their
families.

One night, she remembers, Charles St. Hill had a
visit from a friend who talked about the job he had
lost that day. He had had a fight with a white man he
worked with, and he was fired. The prospects for finding another job right away were not good; it had taken
him a long time to find this one. The two men continued
to talk, and young Shirley, pretending not to listen,
opened her ears. Charles St. Hill was saying that racial
discrimination was keeping him from advancing, too.
He was sick of it. The two neighbors talked some more,
and when the evening was done, they went back to
their lives as they had been and hoped for something
better to come. But Shirley began to have thoughts
that would affect the course of her life.

Soon after that evening, the family made another
move, this time to a housing project on Patchen
Avenue. Shirley left Public School 144 and enrolled in
Public School 28, and then in Junior High School 178,
which was to become part of the embattled Ocean
Hill-Brownsville school district.

Within the year, the family moved back to Ralph
Avenue, but the old tenement building had now been
replaced by a new city housing project, the Kings-
borough Houses, and they settled there for a while.
During this time, Shirley entered Girls' High School at
Nostrand Avenue and Halsey Street, where she continued to excel as a student.

She had a photographic memory and a near-genius IQ. She was a member of Arista, the academic honor society, and was known throughout the school for her scholarship. Her leadership ability, however, did not come out here. She was shy and self-conscious of her West Indian accent. When she spoke, people would laugh and snicker. So all the knowledge she had stored in her head, which turned out to be a considerable amount, she kept to herself. She became a voracious reader, going through as many as ten books a month.

Her teachers were well aware of her potential ability, and they began to prepare her for college. They called in her parents and told them not to worry about money. Shirley would almost certainly win a scholarship, they said. She won four.

She wanted to go to school out of town, where she could live on a campus, meet new people, and be free of the responsibility of caring for her sisters. But there was a cold reality—money. Despite the family's heroic efforts to save, it was still poor. While scholarships covered tuition, they did not cover clothing, living costs, and traveling back and forth from school to home on holidays and during vacations. These seemingly little things can add up to a sum equal to the cost of college tuition, if not more. Then, too, the St. Hills had to think also of the education of their three younger girls.

So, reluctantly, Shirley compromised and entered Brooklyn College in September, 1942.

Brooklyn College is one branch of the City University of New York, a free college system that has provided a chance at higher education for thousands upon thousands of bright but poor young New Yorkers. Tuition is free for full-time day students. Over the years, admissions requirements have become more demanding because of the large numbers of students wanting to enter. In recent times the university has been accused of excluding all but the most gifted black and Puerto Rican students through an admissions policy requiring high-school averages close to ninety percent. In Shirley's day, entrance was determined by passing an examination.

Brooklyn College has trees and large old buildings. It resembles a large college campus upstate or in the Midwest in every way but one—dormitories. Students travel back and forth from school every day.

At Brooklyn, Shirley majored in sociology, but she also concentrated on education and Spanish. Again she won a reputation for being a bookworm.

"There were no parties for me," she recalls. In the spirit of her grandmother's teachings, she spent many long hours in the library. "I saw college as an opportunity for a good education and a chance to make something of myself."

She joined the Harriet Tubman Society for Negro History, which was named for the escaped slave who, as the leading "conductor" of the Underground Railroad, led more than three hundred slaves to freedom. Shirley also joined the debating society.

She began to speak out on social problems, like the effect of World War II, then being fought, on American life. She also talked about racial disorders, raging in the cities at that time, just as they would be in the 1960's. Students and teachers began to take notice.

They saw that she could not be moved from a position, if she knew she was right. They saw her ability to influence other people, even those who disagreed with her. They saw her gift for holding an audience with a fast, almost hypnotic speaking voice.

Her professors tried to convince her to consider a career in politics. But at that time she wasn't interested. She couldn't help thinking of those black politicians of the Reconstruction era who were tools in the hands of powerful white men. She also knew she had two political liabilities. She was black—and she was a woman.

So, upon her graduation in June, 1946, she turned instead to what she thought she could do best, teaching young children. With her well-stocked mind, her frail body, and the face of a fifteen-year-old, she went forth to find a job. She was about to find out for herself exactly what Charles St. Hill's friend had been talking about that night on Ralph Avenue.

Chapter 3

Game Enough to Try

In June, 1946, Shirley Chisholm's face was young, eager—and black. She watched the white students who had graduated with her find jobs they wanted. While she, an honor student with a fine all-around record, was turned down time and time again.

She pounded the pavement, knocking on any door that held even the slightest promise behind it for a job as a nursery-school teacher. Many opened, but then were shut in her face. She had already enrolled in a master's degree program at Columbia University's Teachers College, and she could not even find a job to begin practicing the skills she had learned.

Finally, she heard of a possible opening at the Mount Calvary Methodist Church Nursery School at 140th Street and Edgecombe Avenue in Manhattan. This is in a part of Harlem called Sugar Hill, the home of more affluent blacks, especially entertainers and professional people. Sugar Hill lies north and west of the heart of

Harlem. Just east, on the other side of Seventh Avenue, Harlem's main boulevard, is the area first settled by blacks. That was in the early decades of this century, but even by 1946 that section was deteriorating. Then as now, the community's business and entertainment center was farther south, on 125th Street.

The director of the Mount Calvary Nursery School, Mrs. Eula M. Hodges, was looking for a teacher to care for preschool children. Mrs. Hodges liked to give the impression that she was tough and stern, which she was. But a good deal of the toughness was intended to test people, to find out if they had the guts and nerve to fight back. After her first meeting with this short, stout, firm, and kind woman, Shirley was a little uneasy. But she had seen the same toughness before in her mother and her grandmother.

"You look so much like a child yourself," Mrs. Hodges told her. "Are you sure you can handle a classroom?"

"I am sure," Shirley replied.

"Well, I think we may be able to use you, but you'll have to come back for more interviews before I finally decide," Mrs. Hodges said.

This was another one of Mrs. Hodges's tests. The school director wanted to know her teachers pretty well before making the final decision to hire. This would often mean a series of telephone calls to ask more questions or get their opinions on school matters. But Shirley did not have a phone. To keep in touch she had to keep coming back—day after day, taking three subway trains and riding more than an hour from Brooklyn to Manhattan.

"She would just keep on coming," Mrs. Hodges recalls today. "I just admired her determination. So I asked her, 'Are you sure you want that job?' She said she did, so I told her, 'Well if you're game enough to try, I'm game enough to try you.'"

Shirley was hired and assigned to a group of four-year-old preschoolers. She quickly proved to be a good choice. She sang well. She played the piano and taught the children songs with dances to go with them, like the horse trot, the duck walk, and the elephant run.

She loved to embroider, and when she had older students, she taught them how to sew skirts and embroider designs around the hem. She often wrote plays for the children to act in. It was not long before she was a favorite of the children and adults alike.

As time went on, Shirley and Mrs. Hodges became comfortable with each other. They developed a mutual respect that deepened during Shirley's seven years at Mount Calvary. Mrs. Hodges taught Shirley organization and tried to instill in her a flexibility which she at first feared her young teacher lacked.

"She was always walking around writing things in a little black book," Mrs. Hodges recalls. "I told her, 'Shirley, you never learned that from me. Relax a little.'"

Shirley learned quickly what Mrs. Hodges had to teach her and also showed the director a few things. Each month, the teachers had to present progress reports on their classes at a meeting of the school's board of directors. All the other teachers would read theirs. But Shirley would write her report, carry it to the lectern, and never look at it. She did it all from memory, which proved excellent training for politics.

As she gained more experience, she was given more

responsibility. She left the preschool program and was put in charge of an afternoon group of school-age children.

Each afternoon at three o'clock, Shirley and her fellow teacher, Mrs. Margaret Ormsby, would go to Public School 5 to meet the children and take them back to Mount Calvary. Shirley was thin and had bow legs, even then. As she would lead the children down the street, they would try to imitate her walk, and she would laugh as hard as anyone.

She also got on well with most of the teachers at the school. When they organized a bridge club, Shirley provided the name, *Les Femmes Gaies* (The Lively Ladies).

"She didn't know a diamond from a club when we started, but she soon became an expert player," Mrs. Ormsby recalls.

It was while at Mount Calvary that Shirley was introduced to a Jamaican named Conrad Chisholm. She was short and thin; he was short and plump. His handsome round face would always light up when he smiled, which was much of the time. She liked him for being a good story-teller and a spiffy dresser, and he became the only man Shirley would allow to pamper and try to protect her. She was the prim little school teacher; he was the tough private detective. They had things in common, like Brooklyn, where they both lived, and dancing—they were both accomplished ballroom and Latin dancers. She called him "Raddy," and he called her "one hundred pounds of nuclear energy." Their courtship was filled with laughter and teasing, and in a short time they decided to marry. That was in 1949. The other teachers at the school were delighted at the news and arranged a bridal shower at Mrs. Ormsby's house a few weeks before the wedding.

The night before the wedding, the teachers planned a decorating party at the church where the ceremony and reception would be held. That evening, they worked from nine o'clock until three o'clock the next morning under the tireless direction of Mrs. Hodges.

After the honeymoon, the newly married couple rented a small apartment in Bedford-Stuyvesant. Shirley returned to teaching. For leisure, she and Conrad would sometimes take a trip to Saratoga, New York, to see the horse races. Once a week, *Les Femmes Gaies* played bridge, and when they finished, the men would come to collect their wives or girl friends and to eat the meal that the women would prepare for them.

Over the years, Shirley advanced at Mount Calvary, and by 1952 she was assistant director. She felt ready to tackle a bigger job and applied for the position of director at a small, private nursery in the Brownsville area of Brooklyn.

It was called the Friends-in-Need Nursery, which was a deceptive title. The name implies that it was a school for poor children. It had once been, but not any more. It was one of the oldest nursery schools in Brooklyn and had for long served the children of professional men—doctors and lawyers.

But in the course of time, it had suffered from bad administration, and had gotten into difficult times. Out of desperation, Shirley explains, the board of directors

decided to try letting a black woman run it. Some of the
board members were less happy about the idea than
others.

Once she had joined the school, the parents liked her.
They liked how she did things and the way she was
able to create a good relationship with the people she
worked with. The children especially loved her.

But the board of directors was another matter. Every
month, this group of matronly women would meet on
the third floor of the school. The members would sit in
a large circle, in the middle of which was a table and
chair. When the board members had finished most of
their discussion of school business, they would summon
Shirley by ringing a little bell. And she would have to
take her seat in the center of the circle amid all those
searching and none-too-friendly pairs of eyes.

But instead of asking for her report of the past
month's events at the school, they probed into her personal life. They were always asking her questions about
her husband and her home.

One day, Shirley had had enough. "I think it's ridiculous for me to sit in the center of the circle as if I were
on display," she told them. "From now on, you are to
find me a seat within your circle."

The women were shocked.

"When you work for someone," one of them said to
her, "you do what you are told. There are just some feelings that you should keep to yourself."

"There are," replied Shirley Chisholm, "certain things,
such as pride and dignity, that an individual never gives
up."

She had hoped they would learn to treat her with

some measure of respect, but she finally decided that
the situation could not go on much longer. She now felt
that the supervisory experience she had gained at
Mount Calvary and in her year at the Friends-in-Need
Nursery qualified her for a job with more responsibility.
She registered with the professional-services division of
the New York State Employment Agency. They were
impressed with her, and she seemed right for several
good jobs that the agency had been asked to help fill.

But each time she arrived for an interview, the person doing the hiring would take one look at her face and
find some excuse not to accept her. Often it was the
same person who had just been enthusiastic talking to
her over the telephone. Of course, no one could tell by
her voice that she was black. Even her West Indian
speech pattern didn't tell them anything. Some thought
she was British; others thought she was from Boston.

One day in particular that Shirley Chisholm remembers, she was sent for an interview at a private school
in the Riverdale section in the northwest Bronx. The
state agency representative had told the school that the
applicant knew Spanish well, was an excellent dancer,
and had first-rate credentials.

"Send her right over," the director of the school had
said.

So she got on the subway and took the long ride to
Riverdale. In the early 1950's it was a beautiful, almost
rural area, thick with tall shade trees and spacious mansions, the homes of some of the city's wealthiest and
most influential citizens. Today it houses many upper-
middle-class families in high-rise apartment buildings.
At that time, the only blacks in the area were domestics.

"As soon as I saw the neighborhood, I knew I was doomed," Shirley Chisholm recalls. "It was beautiful, and I knew it was too good for black people. They would never let me have it. I felt it was just a waste of time to me, but I decided to see it through—just to satisfy my curiosity.

"I walked in. I was well dressed. I saw a receptionist sitting there and stood in front of her, waiting for her to acknowledge me. She didn't. Finally, I spoke, and she said:

" 'What do you want?'

" 'I'm here for an interview for a position as a teacher.'

" 'What?' the receptionist replied.

" 'The New York State professional office sent me.'

" 'Oh, you're Mrs. Chisholm,' the woman said. 'I'm so sorry. Please take a seat and I'll tell the director that you are here.' "

The woman left the reception desk for about three minutes, and then returned. Shirley is certain that she went to prepare the director for the shock.

"You have an excellent background, Mrs. Chisholm," he told her when she was finally asked into his office. "But I'm afraid we need someone with a bit more administrative experience."

"No, sir!" she replied. "You're not looking at my credentials at all. Be honest! You didn't know I was black until your receptionist told you. I can tell by the manner in which you gave that little speech. You didn't know my color until I came here, and you were floored no end. You don't have to bother telling me any more lies. Good luck to you."

And she walked out.

She got on the train and headed back to Brooklyn.

"At that point I began to feel that if the day would come when I would ever be able to reach out—White America, look out! I said to myself, White America, you are going to pay for this day!"

And, slowly, she began to join community organizations as a means of venting frustration, but her full development as an active social reformer was to come later. She was still involved in trying to find a job that was more suited to her executive abilities, and she headed back to the New York State office.

"There is a job," she was told, "but I think it has already been filled. I think the man should see you anyway, so I'll call him."

The interviewer made the call, and once again Mrs. Chisholm was told, "Come right over."

This time the position was the directorship of the largest day-care center in the city. It was part of the Hamilton-Madison Settlement House, a community-service agency on New York's Lower East Side. This neighborhood has traditionally been the home of the city's poor, the first stopping place for one wave of immigrants after another—Eastern Europeans, Jews, Puerto Ricans. The streets are crowded with humanity, tenements, and open markets, like those on Essex and Delancey Streets. Poor schools and poor health services are facts of life there.

"I just had a feeling that I would get this job, no matter who had applied," she recalls now. And she did. The center's director, Geoffrey Wiener, liked her record. But more than that, he liked what she was saying.

For six years, from 1953 to 1959, she worked happily

and successfully as supervisor of a teaching staff of twenty at Hamilton-Madison House. The staff was responsible for teaching and counseling 140 preschool children of working parents. She found or made the time for personal interest in all the children, going out of her way to help even in matters not directly related to her official position. Their problems, she soon saw, were the problems of the poverty community, and to help them she became active in neighborhood groups on the Lower East Side. She was no stranger to such problems, having lived them all her life in Brooklyn.

"Shirley never had an easy time of it because she was so principled," Wiener recalls of those years. "She never moved an inch, especially if it was in the interest of the children or their families. She had the character for social work. That profession keeps you tied to reality. Reality is often very unpleasant, and people try to duck it. She helped people see that they could not duck out or escape."

After her six years at the Hamilton-Madison Settlement House, Shirley Chisholm was wooed away by the child-guidance division of the New York City Board of Education, and then by politics.

Chapter 4

The Road to Albany

In 1959, Shirley Chisholm began her new job with the Bureau of Child Guidance for the New York City Board of Education. She worked as a consultant, visiting schools to see how well they were helping students to plan their futures and solve their personal problems. She gained a reputation for being tough and thorough.

But now her growing interest was politics. Her involvement with the Lower East Side community at the Hamilton-Madison Center made her realize the importance of community action.

She had joined the board of directors of the Albany Houses, a city housing project in her own neighborhood of Bedford-Stuyvesant. She attended community meetings and set up youth programs for the children who lived in the Albany Houses. She petitioned for better postal service, for better sanitation, and for solutions to a host of other problems faced by residents of the area.

Five years earlier, she had heard about a political rebel, a man who just would not do what he was told. His name was Wesley McD. Holder. He was a tall, quiet-looking man, partly bald, with light-frame glasses. He never raised his voice, but he too was fierce. By day, he worked as a statistician in the office of the district attorney of Kings County, which is another name for Brooklyn. But at night, he headed an organization called the Bedford-Stuyvesant Political League.

The year before, "Mac" Holder had become the first black person in Brooklyn to beat the powerful Democratic party. His league challenged the regular party organization, ran a black man for a judge's job, and won. While there were many blacks in Brooklyn, very few had been active in politics, and of these, the independent thinkers and the activisits had had little or no chance of getting into office.

It takes money to run a campaign, and candidates usually get financing through their party. Once the party gives an endorsement, the organization's friends and supporters are willing to contribute money to its candidates.

But the Bedford-Stuyvesant Political League was independent. It did not want money from the established local party. The only black elected official the regular organization had ever run for office was Assemblyman Bertram Baker in 1948, and at that time he was considered politically safe. So the league ran its own candidate for the judgeship. Shirley Chisholm, always mindful of the lessons of Reconstruction politics, had heard about the successful effort, and that is why she wanted to join the league. Her formal entry into traditional

politics was through a group that was completely un-
traditional.

"I realized at that time that there were only two ways
to achieve creative change for black people in society—
either politically or by open, armed revolution," she
says about her thinking then.

"Malcolm X, the great black man who was slain in
the mid-1960's, said the same thing later very succinctly
—we must have the ballot or the bullet. Since I also
believe that human life is valuable and important, I decided that for me it would be through the creative use
of the ballot.

"People often ask me how I managed to burst on the
national political scene so quickly. What most fail to
realize is that in Brooklyn there have been black people
working toward political freedom for over twenty years.
They do not realize that political groups in all the
Bedford-Stuyvesants of this country have been strug-
gling, organizing, collecting money to fight toward freedom from white political control of black communities."

With her new political affiliation, Shirley Chisholm
began to work even harder in her community. In the
evenings and on weekends, she was asked to give talks
to church and community groups, and she did so, each
time impressing the audience with her great speaking
ability. She developed more self-confidence.

But she also did the menial work of an organization
member. She stuffed and addressed envelopes during
political campaigns. She went from door to door in the
neighborhood to convince residents to sign petitions or
donate money. She manned the telephones, calling to
get out the vote.

After four years, she felt she was ready for more executive responsibility, and she challenged Mac Holder for the presidency of the league.

"How dared she think she could beat me," the skilled political strategist now recalls in mock outrage. "I warned her not to try it. But she was stubborn and just had to make the effort. I fixed her. I beat her good. And that calmed her down for a while."

But not for long. Shirley Chisholm did not take on Mac Holder in her next big battle, but she decided to fight the organized political machine of Brooklyn.

It occurred to her one day that while it was fine to be a maverick, she should also know what was happening inside established politics. It was part of her general philosophy of trying to work with everyone, while keeping her own integrity and determination to fight for the things she felt were important. But there was no harm, no heresy, in trying to talk to the enemy, so she decided to go and join the local Democratic club.

Rather than make an appointment to meet the head of the organization, she waited for an "open night" at the club. These were periodic meetings during which district leaders opened the doors to anyone in the community who had a problem on the local level, such as housing, welfare, civil service jobs, or postal service. The politician, after all, is supposed to have influence with people who can solve such problems. And on these nights, the leaders tried to show the community how powerful they were. The population of this community was eighty-two percent black. The club was largely Jewish and Irish.

The meeting was held on the second floor of a storefront building. In the front of the room, behind a big table, sat the leaders. One wall of the huge room was lined with white people from the district. The other side was lined with black people. The leaders seemed to call only upon people known at the club to present their problems. It took little time for Shirley to see that the leaders seemed hardly to care about the problems. She was even more surprised when she overheard some women who had been members of the club for as long as fifteen years complaining about the way things were being run.

After the meeting, she invited these women home with her to Sterling Place to talk about what they could do to make the club more responsive to the community. No one's voice, they told her, could be heard unless the leaders wanted to hear it or wanted it to be heard. There was, she said to herself, no system of developing new leadership, and she just did not like it.

"Why haven't you done something about this all these years?" she asked.

"It's no use," they said. "We can't say anything. They will throw us out."

"Well, I think this should be fought. Tell you what. At the next meeting, I'll raise an issue, any issue, just to challenge the position of the chairman. And I expect you to give me support."

When the next business meeting date arrived, Shirley and her small conspiracy went to the club and took their seats along with the other members and visitors. The minutes from the previous meeting were read. Attendance was taken. For a while, anyway, it was business as usual. Then Shirley raised her hand, was recognized, and asked a question about a current controversial issue. Today she can no longer remember what it was she asked about. But it was unimportant compared with the effect that her asking had on the leaders.

"You are out of order, miss. Please sit down," the chairman said to her.

But she would not sit down.

"What's the matter?" she persisted. "Are you afraid of a little opposition?"

The exchange continued, and pretty soon the other women began to speak up and demand some answers. By then, the meeting had turned into bedlam, and the chairman pounded his gavel and called for adjournment.

Not knowing immediately what to do with this woman, the district leaders tried a tactic that is often used to tone down mavericks. It is called *co-optation*. The very next week, Shirley Chisholm received a letter from the district leader inviting her to become a member of the club's executive committee. At first she felt she could not do that. But she reconsidered. She knew the invitation was only an attempt to get her to be quiet. The leaders seemed to believe that, as a member of the ruling body, Shirley would have to go along with the majority. They were wrong.

She went to the next executive-committee meeting and was elected to the post of second vice president. The committeemen felt better, but not for long. Shirley continued to challenge them publicly at meetings, and finally she was voted out of office.

They thought that this would get rid of her, but at the very next public meeting, she was back in the

audience among the women agitating for change. Because the club leadership had never run into anyone
who stood up to them this way, they called her "an
enigma"—a very puzzling person. Slowly, her influence in the club grew stronger as black people in the
community began to realize that she was speaking for
them.

But she was still hampered. Eventually, she helped
form the Unity Democratic Club in 1960. It began to
run candidates against the machine, and became in-
creasingly successful at it. "Our group just could not
stand white people controlling a community that was
mostly black," she explained when asked why the club
was formed.

Conrad Chisholm, who always felt that his wife
could handle herself, began to get a little worried. She
was making some powerful enemies, and she was always
running, running, running, and never getting any rest.
She was almost never at home. If she was not working,
she was at a meeting. And if she was not there, she was
probably ringing doorbells for one cause or another.

Fortunately, they understood each other's habits and
were able to arrange their home life in a way that was
satisfactory to both. This became more important as
Shirley became more prominent in politics. There was
no competition between them. Conrad says he decided
very early in their marriage that there would be only
one star, and his wife would be it. Instead, he would
spend his time making certain her needs were met and
having a good time himself.

He never had the feeling, as many men do, that a

woman's place is in the home and that she should stay there and cook and clean and care for him, especially since they had no children.

Because Shirley has always been a fighter for women's rights, this kind of man appealed to her. He loved to cook, and she did not. So he often prepared very tasty meals. She, on the other hand, liked to clean house and iron. Ironing, she said, gave her time to think. So with this division of labor, the two of them got along. Shirley moved farther away from education and into politics. Conrad eventually left private investigating to become a senior investigator for the city's Department of Social Services, in charge of Medicaid applications.

During this time, the other three St. Hill girls were finishing their education—two of them winning scholarships. In 1945, Charles St. Hill had decided he could use some of his savings for a down payment on a house on Prospect Place in Bedford-Stuyvesant. It was a family house, a small building with several apartments upstairs, one of which eventually went to Shirley and Conrad. There was a garden in the back, where Charles St. Hill, who was getting on in years, loved to work each morning.

One summer day in 1964, when Shirley was on her way to work, she stuck her head out of the window and watched her father, bent over with a spade in his hand, loosening the earth around some flowers. His white hair looked like a patch of snow in the hot summer sun.

"Pop, shouldn't you put a hat on your head?" she called down. "The sun is awfully hot."

"No, Shirls," he called back. "I'll be okay. You go on to work."

But something kept her from going just yet. She walked down to the garden to talk to him some more.

"You know I've always believed in you," he told her. "You have spirit and fight that will take you a long way. Your sisters are nice girls, good girls, but they are not socially minded like you are. Stay that way, Shirls."

And with that she left for work. When she got home that afternoon, she learned that Charles St. Hill had died of a stroke.

Shirley took the news terribly. She and her father had been very close. He had been her model of a man who fought for what he believed in and worked hard to get it. He never stopped trying, even when things were at their worst, and she loved him for being that way and for teaching her to be that way. Because he had believed in Shirley more than he did in his other daughters, he had made her the sole beneficiary of his $10,000 life-insurance policy. Her sisters were furious and from that time stopped talking to Shirley.

Shirley was depressed. Seriously depressed. She could not go to work for a week. All she could think about was her father.

"Pop wouldn't want me to be this way," she told herself over and over again. "I have to snap out of it." Finally, she did and went back to her old job with more energy than ever before.

At that point, in 1964, things came together that allowed her to take her next step up the political ladder. The state assemblyman from her district, Thomas R. Jones, was leaving the state capital in Al-

bany for a seat on the civil court bench in New York
City. Jones had been one of the Unity Democratic
Club's candidates. His stepping down created an opening in the assembly. Shirley Chisholm told her fellow
members of the Unity club that she wanted it.

When the news got around, it did not go over too
well in Brooklyn political circles. The assembly seat
was a desirable job, usually reserved for lawyers who
had faithfully served their party. Most of the men in
the assembly and in the state senate, the other branch
of the New York state legislature, could still maintain
private practices in addition to their law-making duties.

"You are a one-hundred-pound schoolteacher who cannot stand the rigors of politics," the men told her.

Shirley would not listen. "People have an image of
women in politics as heavy-bosomed and middle-aged.
I was fragile, forty years old, and looked younger. My
male colleagues weren't fighting me when they saw me
because they thought I was going to be an easy-going
type. They were wrong."

Using her father's insurance money and all the fight
she could muster, she campaigned hard and became
the Democratic candidate for the seat. As a result, the
Unity Democratic Club strengthened its position. In
November, Shirley Chisholm won election to the two-
year term of assemblywoman and became the second
black woman to serve in the state legislature. The first
had been Bessie Buchanan of Harlem in the 1950's.
After the election, Shirley Chisholm thought she could
just concentrate on doing a good job in state government. But in 1965, because of a court ruling that redrew
the boundary of her district, she had to run again. And

the next year there was still another such ruling. She
had to campaign for the same seat three times in three
years. Each time she was elected by an overwhelming
number of votes. The politicians might not have been
sure about Shirley Chisholm, but the people were.

And she gave her district a kind of representation
that had rarely been seen in Albany. Assemblymen had
to stay in the state capital at least three nights a week,
and many of them did their behind-the-scenes work
over dinner and drinks in the bars of the city. But
Shirley does not like to drink, and she does not like
drunks, even social drunks. Besides, a large number of
her colleagues reminded her of the clubhouse leaders,
and she just could not get along with them. So she went
to her hotel room and did her homework. She read all
the proposed legislation. She studied all the background material her staff had prepared to help her
make her decisions. On the floor of the assembly, she
refused to vote along the established party lines, and
she made enemies. The biggest of these was Stanley
Steingut, the head of Brooklyn politics and the assembly's minority leader.

Shirley picked the issues she would fight for. There
was the SEEK program, designed to get more black
and Puerto Rican students into the City University.
She supported abortion-law reform, unemployment insurance for domestic workers, aid to day-care centers,
and the restriction of weapons' use by policemen. And
she stood by her choices.

One of the big issues in the assembly at this time was
the "Save LIU" drive, and Shirley was right in the
thick of it. LIU is Long Island University, privately

run, with 20,000 students spread over four campuses. The newest of these are C. W. Post College and Southampton College, both in the Long Island suburbs. In downtown Brooklyn were the Brooklyn College of Pharmacy and the Brooklyn Center, where LIU began. The school had opened in 1927 with several hundred students. Over the years the university and its enrollment had grown steadily.

But in 1967, the university's board of trustees announced plans to sell Brooklyn Center to the City University because it would not have enough money to operate in a few years. Tuition had been rising steadily, and—the trustees said—it was just about at the top limit the students could pay.

The students and faculty were outraged. They argued that the sale would deprive the city of a school that served a need not served by the City University. Many of the students at LIU would not have been able to get into the City University. LIU was smaller, the faculty said, and able to give the students more individual attention.

A coalition of those opposed to the sale called up the state assembly's Education Committee, headed by Assemblyman Joseph Kottler, and the committee came to Brooklyn for two weeks of hearings. One committee member who never missed a meeting was Shirley Chisholm. Looking calm and quiet, she sat on the stage of the New York City Community College auditorium, where the hearings were held. A steady stream of students came to the meetings to speak. Then the faculty members came. The representatives from the black community of Fort Greene, nearby to Brooklyn Center, came and pleaded with the committee to stop the sale. The school, they said, had set up programs for neighborhood children and was helping to improve their chances of going to college. Shirley did not say very much during these first few days. When she did, there were cheers.

Under the threat of a court subpoena, John H. McGrath, chairman of the LIU board of trustees, was called to testify. John McGrath was an experienced political diplomat, a man with a soft voice, a ruddy complexion, and a manner that seemed as if he could remain unshaken in a hurricane. For years he had practiced as a lawyer, eventually moving into banking and finance. He was president of the East New York Savings Bank. But he was also one of the most powerful unelected politicians in Brooklyn. Before becoming president of the savings bank, he had held a number of appointed posts, including the chairmanship of the New York State Waterfront Commission. He was a friend of Stanley Steingut, and that made him an enemy of Shirley Chisholm. He was, in short, everything she was fighting against in this business called politics.

As John McGrath took the stand, there were hundreds of LIU students and teachers in the auditorium to witness the confrontation.

The cross-examination began—first Assemblyman Kottler, then Shirley Chisholm, and finally Assemblyman Anthony Mercurello, an alumnus of LIU. At first McGrath stayed cool. He was questioned about the financial status of the Brooklyn Center. Then he was asked why money from this formerly viable institution had been siphoned off to build the university's Long Island campuses. The exchange became more heated. When the legislators charged that he was fleeing Brooklyn for the suburbs and killing the Brooklyn Center in the process, McGrath finally blushed. He retorted that the downtown campus could not be viable for much longer. Before he left the stand, Shirley had called for an examination of the LIU books.

After a day of testimony, students and representatives of the surrounding Fort Greene community stormed the microphone. They were concerned about their future education. Assemblywoman Chisholm sensed the uneasiness and took the opportunity to put some minds at rest.

"I wanted to make a very brief statement with respect to a number of questions that have been directed from the black students in the audience and the community members who have come forward," she said.

"It is my personal belief that there has to be a complete restructuring of the entire educational system. The pressure has got to be borne and put on by community forces. I know how frustrated you are, my brothers and sisters. But I can tell you that as one of your representatives, I am trying in my own small way to bring about some kind of redemption."

Although the two weeks of hearings had been frustrating, they were not fruitless. City University officials had second thoughts about their offer to buy the Brooklyn Center campus. Finally, they withdrew the bid. They stated that they would not participate in ruining a still-useful institution of higher learning.

But the damage had been done. Many faculty members continued to leave the campus. Fewer and fewer new students applied for admission. Brooklyn Center has never been the same since that time.

Chapter 5

This Job
Belongs to a Man

There was great excitement in Brooklyn in the winter of 1967 when a federal court ordered the state legislature to create the Twelfth Congressional District. Throughout the nation, legislatures were redrawing the boundary lines of voting districts to provide a fairer balance of representation. New York's Twelfth brought together ten assembly districts that had been part of other congressional districts. Most of them were in Bedford-Stuyvesant, the largest black community in the borough, ridden with slums but also containing some well-kept private homes. The new unit took in portions of Williamsburg, the area just across the Brooklyn Bridge from Manhattan, with a largely Puerto Rican population; East New York, once the center of New York's Orthodox Jewish community, but now predominantly black; and Bushwick, which is close to the docks and has the most white residents of all these areas. About seventy percent of the new district was black or

Puerto Rican. The rest was Polish, Jewish, Ukrainian, and Italian. There was another relevant statistic about the new district, and Shirley Chisholm was one of the few people aware of it—it contained perhaps thirteen thousand more registered women voters than men.

There was no past history to guide the political leaders in the new district. There was no incumbent—someone already holding the congressional seat—to run for re-election or to choose a successor. There was no certainty even about which party had the majority. But it was pretty well known that most of the time the Democrats won in Brooklyn, as they did in much of the city. The Republicans in New York ran second in most areas. The Liberal party, when it picked its own candidate—rather than endorsing another party's choice—usually ran third. In recent years another political alliance, the Conservative party, had shown some strength. One thing that everyone agreed on was that the voters in the new district would elect a black candidate.

. For the Republicans, opportunity suddenly stepped forward in the person of James Farmer, who had just gotten the nomination of the Liberal party. The Republicans were quick to give him their backing also for the new congressional seat. James Farmer was a nationally known figure, the founding director of CORE, the Congress of Racial Equality. He had participated in the "freedom rides" of the early 1960's, when black people in the South, mostly students, demonstrated for equal accommodations at bus terminals and in public transportation. Farmer had gained a reputation in those days as a fiery speaker and something of a rebel in his own right. But lately, he had settled down. He had taken jobs in established organizations, including a professorship at a small Pennsylvania college. The people of Brooklyn respected James Farmer's record, but there was something about him that they resented badly. James Farmer did not live in Brooklyn. True, he had taken an apartment in the area and had for a year been helping to set up a community college there. But he was an outsider, a carpetbagger.

Assemblywoman Shirley A. Chisholm was making no public statements about the candidacy of James Farmer in the winter of 1967. She was weighing her own political future. By then she had served in the state legislature for three years, and the people of Bedford-Stuyvesant knew her work. They had seen her voting record in Albany and the way she stood up to the bosses. They knew she was an outspoken community leader and had been for nearly twenty years. Now she was trying to decide whether to go after the Democratic party nomination for the new congressional seat. She knew that it would be a fight, that it would be tough, that it would take a good deal of time and energy. The people would support her, she thought, but how could she be certain?

On one of her nights home in Brooklyn, she was sitting and reading when the doorbell rang. At the door she found a delegation of women from the community. They were there to tell her to run for Congress. They had gotten together at one woman's house for coffee and some political conversation. They had taken a vote and decided that they wanted Shirley Chisholm to be their candidate. They did not have much money, they said, because they were all mothers of families on welfare, but they had taken up a collection, each woman donating whatever she could. It came to $9.62. They had placed the money in a crumpled paper bag and brought it right over. That was the moment when Shirley Chisholm decided to run.

The welfare mothers were not the only ones in the community concerned about the new seat that winter. In December, a group of citizens banded together to form the Committee for a Negro Congressman. They would interview the possible black candidates and endorse the one they considered best. Among all the people the committee interviewed, only one was a woman—Shirley Chisholm. Two days before Christmas, a committee spokesman telephoned to give her a present—the committee's endorsement.

The time had come for Shirley Chisholm to talk to the Democratic party leadership in the new Twelfth Congressional District. This consisted of the leaders of the ten assembly districts out of which it had been formed—eight white men and two black. She knew that their main interest was not a candidate who pleased the community. They would prefer someone who they were certain could win and who, once elected, would do what they wanted.

Despite that, Shirley Chisholm approached them and asked for the designation. It would mean the financial and organizational backing of the Brooklyn Democratic party. The leaders told her that it had never entered their minds that a woman should take that seat. Regarding this as merely a delaying tactic, she told them: "After all my years of service, I want the designation. If you don't give it to me, I will fight you for it. You men use a woman for her talents, but when it comes to a position of power, that's a whole different question entirely. I'm not just any woman, either. I have proven skills and abilities that you fail to recognize, and I will fight you."

Still, she tried to convince them that she did not want to run Brooklyn politics. She just wanted an equal chance to run. They said they could not back her, and she said she would show them that the power and money of the traditional machine did not mean everything. She told them that she could beat James Farmer, but they would not listen to her.

The district leaders had another candidate in mind, William C. Thompson, a state senator from the area. He had been a more loyal party member than Shirley Chisholm. That would have won him the nomination, but the district leaders were worried men. They knew that James Farmer was a very strong candidate, almost unbeatable. And they had taken an informal poll in the community and found it heavily in favor of Shirley Chisholm over Senator Thompson. They had to weigh the consequences of supporting a candidate who might not be able to win the votes. They chose a compromise. They would let the district's registered Democrats choose the candidate in an open runoff primary in June.

Shirley Chisholm knew that the party leaders were scared of her, but she also knew that she had a battle on her hands before she could even begin her race against James Farmer. Senator Thompson's standing in the community was good. He was a friend of hers

and could draw support from some of the people and
groups she would have to turn to. Besides that, he
had the local Democratic organization—and its money
—behind him. In addition, there would be still a third
candidate in the June primary, Dolly Robinson, a labor
organizer, also a friend of Shirley, also well known in
the community.

Shirley Chisholm wasted no time; the primary might
be won by the candidate who reached the right people
in the district first. As soon as the primary was announced, she began to telephone old friends, community acquaintances, and ask for their help. "I want
that seat. I have worked hard in the community," she
told them. They knew her, and they knew her work,
and they would help. They began calling others,
building a network of support for her.

One worker decided to hold an organizing and
fund-raising party and to call it "Soul for Shirley." The
menu included fried chicken and spareribs, chitterlings,
collard greens, and potato salad, and there was dancing
and soul music. It was a pretty small gathering—sixty
people—all of whom paid for their dinner and drinks.
It was held in the basement of one of the district's
beautiful private homes. Only $400 was collected that
night. But the purpose of the party was to gather together a group that would support Shirley Chisholm,
people who could contribute more when it was needed,
or who could get out on the campaign trail for her.

At last, Primary Day, June 18, 1968, arrived. The
polls were open from 3:00 P.M. until 10:00 P.M., but
political observers found the turnout disappointingly
small. That night, the tallies were added from all the

voting machines in the new Twelfth Congressional District, and the suspense was ended. Dolly Robinson polled 1,751 votes. Senator Thompson had 4,634. And for Shirley Chisholm there were 5,431. She had won the nomination by fewer than 800 votes.

The primary was over, and the fight was on. As the first order of business, Shirley Chisholm went to Mac Holder, the man from whom she had learned politics. She told him that she could not run without him. She needed him as her campaign manager.

Holder was flattered, but he was also reluctant. He was seventy-one years old. He had retired from politics and was ready for a rest. But he had always been fond of Shirley and admired her fighting spirit. Although he teased her and had fought her when she challenged his leadership in the Bedford-Stuyvesant Political League, he felt that she had the ability and guts to win the election and to get the job done. He had one other characteristic that made him different from most men in politics. He liked to work with women. He believed in them and always did everything he could to help them. In fact, he usually trusted and helped them more than he did men. In a campaign where the issue of sex was certain to come up, Shirley needed a man who felt that way. She knew she could rely on Mac, and she believed in his judgment. He came out of retirement.

The campaign started off with marches through the streets every night and with Shirley paying visits to homes and churches and talking to anyone who would listen. During the day, she and her campaign volunteers would take their sound trucks through the streets of the other assembly districts in the Twelfth Congressional District, where she was not so well known as in her own.

"You don't know me," she would say, "I'm fighting Shirley Chisholm from a neighboring district. I am running for the new congressional seat in the Twelfth District, your district. But the power structure does not want me in Washington, and that is why I am coming to you, the people, so that you can get the message directly. The organization does not want me, but the people do."

This whirlwind campaign was short-lived. Right after the primary battle, Shirley was feeling a little tired and had pain in her abdomen. She took a trip to the doctor to find out what was the trouble, even though she was certain that it was nothing more than a minor irritation. The doctor took one look at her and gave her a good scolding for not coming to him years before. He had discovered a large tumor. If it had been cancerous, she would be as good as dead. He ordered her into the hospital for an operation.

"Please, doctor, not now," she pleaded with him. "It's been there so long, can't we let it stay a little longer? Can't we wait until after the election?"

No, he told her. He reminded her that as a state assemblywoman, she took care of legislative business, and that, as a doctor, he took care of medical business.

"Into the hospital now," he said.

Very reluctantly, and only after Conrad also urged her, she entered the Maimonides Medical Center for surgery on July 18. This was a serious operation. If all went well, she would stay in the hospital about ten days.

Then she would have to rest at home until at least the end of September to regain her strength. The operation would take a lot out of her, too much to allow her to carry on a rigorous campaign schedule. She had her operation, and she came home to rest.

But her opponent, James Farmer, was not resting. He was making his presence felt in the community. Shirley Chisholm's workers were becoming discouraged. They had to work very hard to convince the voters that the rumors were wrong, that Shirley was not dying of cancer. But the longer she stayed off the street, the stronger the rumors got. After all, Shirley Chisholm had made her reputation by being a highly visible public person, and now nobody saw her. The people of Bedford-Stuyvesant were certain that she was dying.

And every day that Shirley Chisholm lay in bed, she would hear her opponent's sound trucks moving through the streets, urging the people to vote for him. Shirley became more and more annoyed until she got what she called "the itch."

"Conrad," she said one day, "the stitches are not in my mouth. They are in my stomach. I can't stand this anymore. I just have to get out and campaign."

"No, Shirley," he replied. "You know what the doctor told you. It's only been three weeks since your surgery. You have lost so much weight. You should take more time to rest."

But she ignored all medical advice and all good common sense as well, following her political sense instead. It told her that she had better get back out there and meet the people or risk losing the election.

She was still weak, but her spirits were stronger than ever. "It was just the therapy I needed," she says, and she felt no pain once she moved back into action.

The whole country was watching this race, and no one, except the people of her district, could understand why this skinny little schoolteacher was taking on such a match.

James Farmer's name was very well known. He was, Shirley Chisholm would always say jokingly, "the national figure." Shirley Chisholm was not. Since his days in the civil rights movement, Farmer had always sought meaningful ways to serve black people. Newspaper editors and other opinion-makers, knowing his background and his desire to find a new dramatic role in the movement, readily endorsed him for the seat. It was, they felt, the least that could be done for a man who had fought so hard and for so long. He was considered so much the favorite in the election that newspaper headlines would read: *Farmer and Woman Debate in Brooklyn Race.* Shirley Chisholm's name was not considered important enough to mention.

But she had come to expect this, and it did not bother her. She relied on her strengths. For one thing, she was an experienced debater. She knew the political ropes probably better than he did—after all, she had campaigned for office before, and he had not. This was her home ground. It was definitely not Farmer's. She had a strong following in church and community groups. And the people knew her firsthand.

During the race, the two candidates would appear at campuses in the area, like Brooklyn College, where the student bodies strongly favored Farmer. But when

Shirley Chisholm discussed the issues—housing, education, welfare reform—a lot of minds were changed. This happened time and again, wherever they debated, at schools, churches, on television. The assemblywoman was a dynamic speaker, and the experts and political professionals had just not counted on that.

Eventually, when all else failed, the issue of man versus woman crept into the campaign. This had nothing to do with a woman's qualifications for the job. It was part of the shadow that had been cast over black people in America since 1966 by the "Moynihan Report." Daniel Patrick Moynihan, who was to become an advisor on urban affairs to President Nixon, was at that time a sociologist at the Massachusetts Institute of Technology. This large and famous scientific school outside Boston had become more and more involved in nonscientific studies, particularly urban affairs. The Department of Labor commissioned MIT to prepare a profile of the black family in the United States, and Moynihan was put in charge of it. His report concluded from the figures sampled that black families are more often run by women that by men. The reason given was that black woman are able to find and keep their jobs better than black men. Moynihan traced this back to the days of slavery, when black women were treated with favor while black men were kept down to prevent slave revolts. Moynihan's report went beyond conclusions and speculations about those conclusions to state that the black family must change if it is ever to be stable and solid. The black communities were angry and upset. But while black people objected to the Moynihan conclusions, there was also great sensitivity to the conditions they were supposed to be based on. In this election of 1968, Shirley Chisholm's opponents believed that electing a black woman to Congress would only help prove Moynihan's point for him.

Shirley knew this argument would not sway the black women who supported her, but she decided to cover all the possibilities. She would go talk to white women, too, especially in Bushwick, home of most of the new district's white voters.

"Honey," she told Conrad one morning, "I have to go to war. I have to let the people know what has to be done to bring change in this country, and I have to take my message to them. I must leave home for three days to go to live in Bushwick. I want to concentrate on the three big housing projects there."

And that's what she did, holding a series of teas and meetings in the living rooms of Bushwick. The women there had backed Senator Thompson in the primary, and Shirley was afraid they would now support James Farmer. She knew what she was doing in a district where there were more women than men and where, proportionately, white voters tended to go to the polls in larger numbers that the blacks.

These teas were in a way a repetition of that coffee gathering of black welfare mothers that started Shirley Chisholm's congressional campaign. In a variety of forms, such parties were a feature throughout the primary and election battles. They served to raise $8,000 in campaign funds.

And the Shirley Chisholm campaign efforts were not restricted to Brooklyn. Fund-raising events were being held in many places. Mrs. Hodges from Mount Calvary organized one in Harlem. Shirley's old friend was quick to answer critics who wanted to know why they were raising money for someone they would not even be able to vote for.

"She's great," Mrs. Hodges would answer the questioners. "If she is elected, her work for Brooklyn will help you, too."

Back in Bedford-Stuyvesant, Shirley Chisholm was still taking nightly walks through the neighborhood, shaking hands and meeting the people, young and old.

James Farmer's people were out, too. Each time Shirley would stop and attract a crowd, the Farmer supporters would come to heckle.

"This job belongs to a man," they would say.

Shirley's campaign workers responded with a new tactic. They would carry with them some of the Farmer campaign literature as well as their own. When Farmer's supporters challenged them, they would take out fliers of both candidates and read what each had to say about the issues.

"See, you can understand what we are saying. Now read his literature. He has to learn the problems of this community. We know them. We've lived them all our lives."

Throughout the heated and highly competitive race, Shirley's campaign people kept coming up with new ideas. They had one in particular that they were saving for the homestretch. Two Saturdays before election day, a caravan of sixty cars snaked through Brooklyn. It was led by a sound truck. In the first car was Shirley Chisholm and behind her were her enthusiastic supporters. They would stop on street corners, at housing projects. Shirley, wearing a dramatic black-and-white cape and the high spiked heels she never tired of, would get out and give her "unbossed and unbought" speech. Her workers would scurry through the crowds, emptying shopping bags full of Shirley Chisholm fliers.

Farmer supporters heard about the motorcade and immediately dispatched their flatbed band truck to stop and play live music wherever the Chisholm caravan had stopped. Shirley's people heard about that, and some went back. "True, they have a band truck, and that is nice," they told the crowds still gathered there. "But we don't have that kind of money. So we are coming to you with the issues, not with music to soothe you. And we hope you will see that we care."

They kept riding around until it was well after dark and only three cars remained, but it had been an exciting day, and they were a happy and confident gang of campaign workers.

It all paid off. On November 5, 1968, Shirley Chisholm won more than twice as many votes as Farmer—35,239 to 13,615.

"Let's find Farmer and show him the way home," one Chisholm supporter shouted. Shirley, smiling and looking relaxed in a green knit suit and her ever-present high heels, accepted the victory flowers quietly.

The year was capped by a Christmas victory dinner in her honor at Brooklyn's Saint George Hotel. A sea of people came, paying fifteen dollars a person. The money helped cover a campaign debt than ran into thousands of dollars, because Shirley Chisholm had refused to accept large contributions from any one source.

It was quite a crowd. There were, of course, the people who had worked closely with her. But many people from the community, who could ill afford the price of the tickets, were there too. So were other congressmen from New York City, and party officials who had been invited only as a political courtesy, with no thought that they would really come.

"We don't agree with the way you conduct politics," they told her. "We don't know how you get away with it, but we admire your spirit and your fight, and we just wanted to let you know that."

Chapter 6

The First Black Congresswoman

Even if Shirley Chisholm had been a quiet, shy person, her arrival in Washington in January, 1969, would have been a major event. She was, after all, the first black woman to be elected to the Congress of the United States, and everyone wanted to see this new breed of politician. Her remarks made them even more curious. Freshman congressmen have never been considered very important in the Washington political establishment. With 435 members in the House of Representatives alone, why should they be? But Shirley Chisholm said she would not be a slave to the congressional seniority system. She would speak her mind and say what she felt was best for the voters of her district and for black people in general.

"Whether a black politician represents an urban, rural, or suburban district, whether he represents a white district, a black district, or a racially split district, there are certain things that he should never

forget. The first is that he is black. And he should
never forget it because his opponents won't forget it,
nor will the electorate."

Ears perked up. Who was this small, frail woman with
the big mouth? She talked very boldly, but what could
she do, everyone wanted to know. Shirley Chisholm's
phone never stopped ringing for appointments for newspaper and magazine interviews, and it seemed as if
there was a dinner invitation for every night. But she
did not accept them, preferring to stay in the one-
bedroom apartment she had rented in Washington and
read and learn about the workings of Congress. She
decided that her battles would not be fought on the
cocktail circuit. She had already rejected that in Albany.
Instead, she would fight in Congress. Four days a week
she would remain in Washington, away from Conrad.
The rest of the week she would be back in Brooklyn or
traveling.

The first month was busy and uneventful—setting
up one office in Washington and another in Brooklyn
for her constituency, hiring a staff, learning her way
around Capitol Hill. Many newspaper and magazine
stories were written about her, but she had not yet
spoken publicly.

Then in March, 1969, she made her maiden speech on
the floor of the Congress. Each representative's first
floor speech is considered his or her maiden speech.
Usually, it draws no more notice than a mention in the
local newspaper back home. Shirley Chisholm's was
different. She was being watched to see what she would
say. And when she finally opened her mouth, it was to
say something explosive.

She said she planned to vote against all money bills for the military or for defense until more was done about poverty at home, and the old politicians shuddered and snickered. "You're committing political suicide," they told her to her face.

"I've been told I've been committing political suicide for fifteen years," was her answer. "I've been told that for so long that as a result I have risen to the top. I don't choose to play by your rules."

It was early in her congressional career that the event occurred that planted Shirley Chisholm firmly on the national scene. It happened because of committees. All congressmen belong to committees, whose job it is to study and vote on proposed laws. The proposals are called bills, and the committee system creates small groups of experts for just about every subject on which the Congress can make laws. Not all the committees are equally important. The major ones, from a congressman's point of view, are those that affect a large segment of the population and those that hand out or control huge sums of money. Membership on the major committees is usually reserved for senior congressmen who have served many years. They are the lawmakers who are supposed to have the experience and judgment to deal with the most important national issues. New congressmen are appointed to less important committees, supposedly to let them learn how the system works.

Shirley Chisholm is an educator. She believed that her twenty years in teaching had given her a particularly good background for making a contribution to the people of this country. It was her hope that she would be appointed to the influential Education and Labor

Committee, of which Adam Clayton Powell had been chairman.

But when the assignments were posted, she found her name listed on the Agriculture Subcommittee on Forestry and Rural Villages. She said this was hardly a place where she could help the most urban area in the world, Brooklyn, New York. She protested.

"The forestry subcommittee has no relevancy whatever to the needs of my constituency. Apparently, all the gentlemen in the Congress know about Brooklyn is that a tree grew there," she said when the appointment was announced. "The Speaker of the House told me to 'be a good soldier.' I told him, 'That's why this country is the way it is today. Everybody's being a good soldier instead of fighting for what is right.'

"True, there are rules and regulations one must follow, but I don't intend to have persons constantly reminding me of protocol. I will be in Congress to fight for a people who have long been denied the opportunity to have their problems and hopes dramatically focused."

She followed that speech with an unprecedented move. The next day, she filed an amendment to the assignments to have her named removed from the committee roll. Finally, she received a letter reassigning her to the Veterans Affairs Committee. She planned immediately to begin investigating discrimination in veterans' groups and to work for improved educational and financial benefits for veterans. She has since then taken part in investigations into the treatment of black servicemen. These came about in the wake of racial disorders on military bases at home and abroad in 1969.

Actions such as these have endeared Shirley Chisholm to people who felt it was impossible to fight the system. But they have made her enemies in the House, enemies who are now intent on hampering her congressional effectiveness.

The southern delegation has not been overfriendly to her, either. One fellow congressman never said a word to her. But each time he would see her walking down the aisle of the House of Representatives, he would pull out a handkerchief and spit into it very loudly. At first, she thought it was a coincidence that he would do this just as she passed, but it soon became clear to her that it was meant as an insult.

One day, she sneaked up behind him with a large man's handkerchief. Before he could pull his out, she spit into hers, making as loud a noise as he had ever made.

"Beat you today," she said with a smile. And he never did that again.

Her reputation for spunk and quick thinking grew. She adopted a following that, she says, embraces all the oppressed people of America—the young, the poor, women, and nonwhites, including blacks, Puerto Ricans, and Indians. As part of her role, she has set out to speak all over the country on their behalf.

Since taking office, she has had more than fifty campus speaking engagements. She has spoken in more than thirty states. The demands on her time have caused her to readjust her weekly schedule. A good part of the time that she used to spend home relaxing on weekends is now given over to traveling and speaking. One rule has remained constant, though—she is always in Washington on Mondays, Tuesdays, and Wednesdays, unless something very special occurs.

"The people of my district elected me to work on their problems in Washington. I owe it to them to be there and not to be running all over the country, leaving their needs unattended," she explains.

"If you don't see me here on the streets, don't worry," she tells people she meets in her district. "It is because I am in Washington working for you."

She realizes how important her voice is for the people who have rarely been heard. Black representatives, she says, have as their constituency all black people, not just those of their districts.

"The one thing I've noticed in my traveling around is the eager reaching out of people. It's frightening to me. I look into faces and see hunger for leadership. I can't get over it. Since I've been on the national scene, it's been like a whirlwind."

That whirlwind has included many different activities, from leading a two-mile march in Harlem on Afro-American Day, September 22, 1969, to signing up as a census taker for the 1970 count. She has to accept awards at luncheons and dinners. She has dozens of plaques lining the walls of her offices in Washington and in Brooklyn, and at home.

When she does get time to relax, she usually stays at the home that she and Conrad bought just after the election. It is a nine-room attached brick building on St. John's Place in the East New York section. One living-room wall is almost completely covered with a large picture of the congresswoman. Most of the furniture is in the rounded, stuffed Victorian style, and there is a large, baby-grand piano, which she plays whenever she gets the chance.

Conrad Chisholm, in the meantime, has become active in politics himself. He has been an election district captain for the Unity Democratic Club.

So Chisholm politics is now a family term. Shirley Chisholm makes it quite clear what that stands for on a number of issues. One of the most important to her is women's rights.

The equal-rights movement for women that has taken hold of this country in the 1970's is an old fight for Congresswoman Chisholm. Her whole life has been a fight against discrimination—directed toward black people or women. In 1969, hers was a strong voice for legislation to grant women equal rights. The Equal Rights Amendment to the Constitution was finally passed in 1970.

"When a young woman graduates from college and starts looking for a job," she told Congress, "she is likely to have a frustrating and even demeaning experience ahead of her. If she walks into an office for an interview, the first question she will be asked is, 'Do you type?'

"There is a calculated system of prejudice that lies unspoken behind that question. Why is it acceptable for women to be secretaries, librarians, and teachers, but totally unacceptable for them to be managers, administrators, doctors, lawyers, and members of Congress?

"The unspoken assumption is that women are different. They do not have executive ability, orderly minds, stability, leadership skills, and they are too emotional.

"It has been observed before that society for a long

time discriminated against another minority, the blacks, on the same basis—they were different and inferior. The happy little homemaker and the contented 'old darky' on the plantation were both stereotypes produced by prejudice.

"As a black person, I am no stranger to race prejudice. But the truth is that in the political world I have far more often been discriminated against because I am a woman than because I am black.

"Prejudice against blacks is becoming unacceptable, although it will take years to eliminate it. But it is doomed because, slowly, white America is beginning to admit that it exists. Prejudice against women is still acceptable. There is very little understanding yet of the immorality involved in double pay scales and the classification of most better jobs as 'for men only.'

"More than half of the population of the United States is female. But women occupy only two percent of the managerial positions. They have not even reached the level of tokenism yet. No women sit on the AFL-CIO Council [the country's most influential organized labor coalition] or Supreme Court. There have been only two women who have held cabinet rank, and at present there are none. Only two women now hold ambassadorial rank in the diplomatic corps. In Congress, we are down to one senator and ten representatives.

"Considering that there are about three and a half million more women than men in the United States, this situation is outrageous. It is true that part of the problem has been that women have not been aggressive in demanding their rights. This was also true of the black population for many years. They submitted to oppression and even cooperated with it. Women have done the same thing. But now there is an awareness of this situation, particularly among the younger segment of the population.

"As in the field of equal rights for blacks, Spanish-Americans, the Indians, and other groups, laws will not change such deep-seated problems overnight. But they can be used to provide protection for those who are most abused, and begin the process of evolutionary change by compelling the insensitive majority to re-examine its unconscious attitudes.

"It is for this reason that I wish to introduce today a proposal that has been before every Congress for the last forty years and that sooner or later must become part of the basic law of the land—the equal rights amendment.

"It is obvious that discrimination exists. Women do not have the opportunities that men do. And women that do not conform to the system, who try to break with accepted patterns, are stigmatized as 'odd' and 'unfeminine.' The fact is that a woman who aspires to be chairman of the board, or a member of the House, does so for exactly the same reasons as any man. Basically, these are that she thinks she can do the job, and she wants to try.

"An argument often heard against the equal rights amendment is that it would eliminate legislation that many states and the federal government have enacted giving special protection to women and that it would throw the marriage and divorce laws into chaos.

"As for the marriage laws, they are due for a sweeping reform and an excellent beginning would be to wipe

the existing ones off the books. Regarding special protection for working women, I cannot understand why
it should be needed. Women need no protection that
men do not need. What we need are laws to protect
working people, to guarantee them fair pay, safe working conditions, protection against sickness and layoffs,
and provisions for dignified, comfortable retirement.

"Men and women need these things equally. To say
that one sex needs protection more than the other is a
male-supremacist myth as ridiculous and unworthy of
respect as the white-supremacist myths that society is
trying to cure itself of at this time."

That was her speech before the Congress. But when
she is on the speaking circuit, she is much more vola-
tile:

"Women must rebel—they must react to the traditional stereotyped education mapped out for them by
society. Their education and training are programmed
and planned for them from the moment the doctor says,
'Mr. Jones, it's a beautiful baby girl!' And Mr. Jones
begins disregarding mentally the things that she might
have been and adds the things that society says that
she must be.

"That young woman will be wrapped in a pink
blanket (pink because that is the color of her caste)
and the unequal segregation of the sexes will have
begun.

"What is so unfair about this is that the major thing
I have learned is that women are the backbone of
America's political organizations. They are the letter
writers and the envelope-stuffers and the telephone-
answerers; they are the campaign workers and orga-

nizers. They are the speech writers and the largest number of potential voters. Yet they are rarely the elected officials.

"The question which now faces us is: Will women in sufficient numbers dare to have an effect on their own attitudes toward themselves and thus change the basic attitudes of males and the general society?

"Women will have to brave the social sanctions in great numbers in order to free themselves from the sexual, psychological, and emotional stereotyping that plagues us. It is not feminine egotism to say that the future of mankind may very well be ours to determine. It is simply a plain fact. The softness, warmth, and gentleness that are often used to stereotype us are positive human values—values that are becoming more and more important as the general values of the whole of mankind are questioned.

"The strength that marked Jesus Christ, Gandhi, and Martin Luther King was a strength born not of violence but of gentleness, understanding, and human compassion."

Strong words, yes. But they are not just words where Shirley Chisholm is concerned.

In April, 1969, twenty-one members of the Black Panther party, a paramilitary revolutionary organization, were arrested in New York City on charges of plotting to bomb and burn department stores. Although they were acquitted two years later, they were held until they could pay $100,000 each in bail, which would allow them to be free until their trial. For ten months, not one member of the group could pay that amount, and they stayed in jail, their trial still not scheduled to begin. Finally, a citizens' group held a benefit and raised bail for one party member. Then clergymen got together about four months later and raised bail for a second party member, a woman.

A third member, another woman, took her case to Shirley Chisholm. Her name was Joan Bird. Before her arrest, she had been studying to be a nurse. She had been arrested on another count just before the bombing charge, and she had been in jail for over a year. She sent Congresswoman Chisholm all the details of her case.

Shirley read the material with interest. She had been concerned about the position of the Panthers, whose stated goal is armed struggle against the United States government.

"It is not the white lawless groups that are having their doors kicked in, it is the Black Panthers," she had said following a series of police raids on Panther offices around the country that resulted in the death of twelve party members. "Skin, skin, skin. That is the criterion for action by the police. It makes us special targets."

So she decided to work actively for Joan Bird, and mapped out a plan. That was in May, 1970.

To carry out her plan, she had to break one of her strictest rules. She did not go back to Washington one Sunday night, but stayed in New York. On that Monday morning she held a press conference. Her announcement was brief and to the point. She said she was heading a coalition of women's groups to raise bail for Joan Bird. This would be a feminine effort, she said, and she knew it would succeed. There were skep-

tics, but within a month the young woman had been
bailed out of jail. Woman Power!

Another issue that has occupied Shirley Chisholm's
time is the repeal of laws against abortion. While still
in the state assembly of New York, she was constantly
fighting for the repeal of the state abortion law. She
was fighting to allow any pregnant women who did not
want to have her baby the right to a safe operation in
a hospital. Since the New York law was among the
strictest in the country, many women who would not
or could not have babies submitted themselves to illegal abortions under filthy conditions, which sometimes
caused death.

Three times while Shirley Chisholm was in Albany,
abortion-law-reform bills were proposed, and she voted
for them. But they did not pass. Meanwhile, other states
around the country were abolishing or liberalizing their
laws. Once she got to Washington, she began advocating national repeal. It was an emotional issue. Religious and community groups opposed abortion as a
form of murder. Shirley Chisholm believed that any
person who did not agree with this opinion should have
the right to end an unwanted pregnancy. There were
many people who agreed with her, including the New
York state legislature, which finally did pass a new law.

She felt that the number of unwanted and illegitimate
births in the country required a more liberal abortion
policy. It was the poor Shirley Chisholm was most concerned about. Even legalization would not solve all
problems; most legal abortions still cost about $400.

But she began to speak out in favor of abortions on television and radio shows, in speeches before civic groups, in Congress. The reply came from desperate women who needed help but did not know where to get it. One letter said:

At last, someone speaks on the subject of abortion from the standpoint of a woman. It is encouraging to hear such a rational statement from a lawmaker, and I hope that you will help change the attitudes of your colleagues.

Another came from a teacher in a junior high school in New York City:

A fifteen-year-old pupil at our school died of an illegal abortion before she ever had a chance to live. The entire school was in mourning. The kids are hysterical and the teachers stunned. How long must this go on? These stupid killer laws must be abolished.

Of course, there are always anonymous crank letters, and this issue brought them out:

I heard your advice on TV last week to women to "storm the gates of the hospitals and demand abortion as their right." As usual your race has the cart before the horse. Why don't you advise these women to storm the family-planning agencies and birth-control clinics and stop these large families of eleven and twelve children, many of them illegitimate. These people can help themselves more than they are doing.

As an educator and a woman concerned with women's

rights, Shirley Chisholm has been fighting hard on another front. She wants the federal government to build
more day-care centers. The demand by working mothers
for friendly places to leave their children during working hours far outreaches the supply. Many mothers who
are not working, welfare mothers who want to work,
she says, are unable to do so because private baby-
sitting expenses eat up all the money they can earn.

"We have thirty-two million working women and
many more who want to work," she testified before a
Senate subcommittee. "We have five million preschool
children, but only six hundred forty-one thousand day-
care spaces available. Many women, approximately
three million, are raising their children in fatherless
homes. Among the black population, one of every four
homes is run by a woman.

"It is just not enough to give day-care payments to
women. It is like giving someone grocery money where
there is no grocery store. We need to spend money, big
money, on facilities and teacher training for day care
if we want our training and employment programs to
work."

The phrase *law and order* has come to have many
meanings on our national scene, and to occupy many
minds, including Shirley Chisholm's. The presidential
campaign of 1968 was run largely on the issue of law
and order. As the phrase was used then, it seemed to
mean that the incoming administration would fight
street crime. But it came to mean that students and
blacks and anyone else who protested in a loud and
sometimes unlawful way had better watch out. It

meant that the Justice Department, which acts as the
federal police department, was not going to stand for
any more nonsense. Shirley Chisholm, like most black
politicians, has been fighting against this kind of law-
and-order politics.

"This country," she has said, "as many of you are no
doubt aware, was founded by aggressive young men
who used violent means because they were necessary
to get change. Now, what did this change involve?

"The Boston Tea Party, for example, can be looked
at from two sides. A member of the 'silent majority' of
that time would probably have characterized them as
'rowdies' or 'vandals,' people who 'upset the system' and
threatened to ruin that majority's indifference to the
people.

"But, if you remember your grade-school history
books, the Boston Tea Party was, in actuality, a patri-
otic and in fact a 'soulful' move; one which by its actions
let everyone know that the average American farmers
and craftsmen, as well as common laborers, were fed
up and tired of a regime which ignored their just complaints and left them no choice but violent political
action. Naturally, they were criticized by the 'responsible' conservatives everywhere.

"The Underground Railroad—that great system of
moving slaves out of the South and into Canada—
was another example of a protest that grew directly
from the 'little men,' the homesteader and the small
homeowner, who combined with the college-trained
intellectuals and their wives against the greatest of all
American insults to humanity—*slavery*. These aboli-

tionists were well aware of the destructive effect of slavery on all aspects of American life.

"It may sound as if I am advocating abolishing government, but I am not. As a duly elected official in that government, I want to talk about changing it.

"The problem in the country now is the threat of an increasing and unlawful force by government, especially the Department of Justice, against citizens. That department is trying by politically motivated actions to reverse the Supreme Court decisions on desegregation of schools and to ignore the court's rulings against using force to make suspected criminals confess to crimes.

"Law and order, they say it is. How tired I am of hearing that phrase. It's not really so new, you know. It comes from Adolf Hitler.

"If my district, Bedford-Stuyvesant, were to have real law and order, then I have no doubt that the people would support it. If law and order meant putting more police on the streets in high-crime, inner-cities areas to cut down street crimes, then I would be yelling the loudest in favor of it. But, my friends, it does not.

"Most funds given to police forces in the name of law and order do not go to those cities with high crime rates. The Omnibus Crime Control Act of nineteen sixty-eight gave money for the police, but much of it went to small-town police departments. Do you know what those towns did with federal tax money? They traded in their nineteen sixty-eight squad cars for nineteen sixty-nines with air conditioning included. They bought tear gas, smoke bombs, mace, and bullets. Bigger cities did the

same thing. But not one police force used its newly
found money to raise the salaries to attract more qualified men and cut down on police accepting bribes from
criminals. These are some of the facts which add to the
rising crime rate."

Shirley Chisholm has also been outspoken on the
Vietnam war.

"I am deeply and unquestionably opposed to the war
in Vietnam," she has said. "I consider it immoral, un-
just, and unnecessary. We have been pouring out the
lives of our sons and wasting the spirit and the re-
sources of our nation to support a corrupt and dicta-
torial government whose citizens would reject it, if
it were not protected by American soldiers.

"President Nixon talks about pulling the troops out.
The secretary of defense talks of helping the Vietnamese
people take over the war themselves, a policy called
Vietnamization. But the talk of both men should be
looked at closely, because it is not what it appears to
be. The pullouts were token numbers of men. Vietnamization is a fraud. It is just a device to keep this
unconstitutional, undeclared, unpopular war going on
and on.

"To show my displeasure with these policies, I intend
to vote against every money bill that comes to the
floor of Congress that provides any funds for the Department of Defense. Any bill whatsoever, until the
time comes when our values and sense of duty to the
citizens is turned right side up again, until our country
starts to use its wealth for people and for peace, not
profits and war."

These are the issues Congresswoman Chisholm takes to the people. And she takes them directly to all the people. Each time she stops in a town, she demands that she be taken to the poor communities so that she can meet and talk with the people.

Her hosts, she says, always try to prevent her from seeing the poverty and unhappiness of these neighborhoods. They do not understand, she adds, that she was once poor, and they are surprised at the welcomes she receives.

"I have my job because the people want me to have it. I serve at their say-so, and if the people really dig you and you have their support, nothing can stop you."

Chapter 7

A Typical Day

Washington

In the early Washington morning, they first become aware of her when they hear the click, click, click of her heels and her quick step on the marble floors of the Longworth House Office Building. Then they see the figure almost glide by, perfectly straight. Only her feet seem to move. The black workmen recognize her immediately and say hello. With a smile, she returns the greeting. Women, mostly secretaries, nod happily in her direction.

It is a short trip from the front door of the large lobby with the high ceiling to the first-floor office of Representative Shirley A. Chisholm, and this little scene is repeated every morning.

Today, May 12, 1970, will be a typical day—busy. But it has many qualities that make it special. This has been a special, sad month. The United States has expanded the war in Southeast Asia by sending troops temporarily into Cambodia, South Vietnam's neighbor to the west. In response to that action, students across the country have been holding large protest demonstrations, and more than fifty schools were closed. During one rally at Kent State University in Ohio, four students were shot by National Guardsmen. This outraged the nation's students even more, and another hundred schools have been closed. Now, two black students have been killed by policemen on the campus of Jackson State College in Mississippi.

A mass depression has set in over the country. This particular morning, the congresswoman plans to see students. But they are not due to arrive until eleven o'clock, and she is using the early hours to talk to her staff and read her mail.

The offices given to freshman members of Congress are not very fancy. There are no scenic views of Washington from the windows. There is no plush carpeting or fancy upholstery. The office is functional. As you come in from the hallway, you see one large room with a table and desks lined up. These are for the staff of four, headed by Mrs. Carolyn Smith who, at thirty-one, is the oldest person there. Also present are six student internes from Colgate University in Hamilton, New York. Colgate is one of the schools that have advanced courses of study in government and send their students to Washington for six months or a year to see how the country is run and to make themselves generally useful. Six are assigned to Representative Chisholm, and they like it so much that twice that number will be back in the fall.

The first order of business is to check with the staff member doing research on the Opportunities Industrial

Centers program, usually known simply as OIC. This is a job-training project for poor youngsters all over the country, with one of the largest units in Shirley Chisholm's own district in Brooklyn. She wants to make this project the model for all job-training programs in the country, and she is preparing a long report for the Senate committee hearing the issue. Her researcher has looked at every state and listed the number of jobs available in each, with the number of unemployed persons living there. From the figures it is obvious that a lot of job retraining will be needed. The congresswoman will include this information in her report.

Next, she tackles the mail to see what the public is asking for or commenting on. One letter is from a small businessman who had asked for help in getting a federal loan. Her staff was able to help him, and he is just letting her know that, thanks to her, he has become a very successful undertaker. A second letter is from a young woman seeking information on where to get an abortion. Shirley Chisholm refers this letter to her staff, which has a national referral system to help in cases of unwanted pregnancy. Another is from the mother of a serviceman who does not want her son to go to Vietnam. It is a typical assortment—a few kind words and happy thoughts, but mostly people in trouble, not knowing what to do about it. Then there are the regular crank letters, which are unceremoniously placed in the "nut file."

One comes from Dothan, Alabama, in response to a speech Representative Chisholm gave urging that the birthday of the Reverend Dr. Martin Luther King, Jr., be made a national holiday:

*We heartily agree with you that the date Martin
Luther King was shot should become a national holiday* [that was not the date she was talking about].
*Since you go to all means seeking publicity, did you
ever consider suicide?*

And there is another from Houston:

*Do you plan to march around our cities raising hell
and having people killed? If you do, you can expect
just what he got. The great silent majority do not
share your views.*

The first has no signature and no return address. The
second is signed with initials and comes from a post-
office box, so it is answered. Shirley Chisholm responds:

*Concerning the silent majority you mentioned, if
your letter is an example of what this silent majority
has to say, it might best remain silent for the good of
all America.*

Enough of that.

Two hours have passed. It is now eleven o'clock, and
the buzzer of the telephone on the large wooden desk
rings. The congresswoman's secretary tells her that her
visitors are here.

"Send them in," she says.

In march a dozen students from Drew University in
Madison, New Jersey. They are upset about the month's
events, and they have come to talk to the one person
they know will understand the way they feel. The small
office has room to seat only six people comfortably on
the long leather couch and one chair. Shirley Chisholm

never refuses to let anyone in for lack of space, so they
squeeze in where they can—standing in corners, sitting
on the floor. And when more come in, they rest gently
on the side of her desk.

The setting is intimate and relaxed. But the students
are a little awed. They don't talk much. They mostly
listen.

She begins by telling them about congressmen who
oppose the war demonstrations and support President
Nixon's policy in Southeast Asia.

The students are very concerned about this, because
most do not want to be drafted into the army to fight.

"Many of the gentlemen in the House of Representatives have sons who are eligible to serve in the Army,
but who are in reserve units," she tells the students.
"The Army Reserve meets only one weekend each
month, and two weeks in the summer. A young man,
if he can find a place in a reserve unit, can serve this
way for six years, with almost no chance of his ever
being called to go to war.

"This just has me burning. I'm just beginning to go
down the list, and as soon as I possibly can, I am
going to see what is going on and begin asking some
questions."

Then she tells them of her fight to get the vote for
eighteen-year-olds. The voting age in most states at
this time is still twenty-one. But within months of this
visit the Senate will pass a law to lower it.

On this particular day, most of the country, and certainly most of the Congress, is against giving young
people the vote. Allowing youth to vote will almost

assure a Republican defeat in the presidential election in 1972, Representative Chisholm tells her student listeners.

"Youth is a positive force in this country. Most congressmen react to the daily diet of television news that only shows college kids throwing eggs at the National Guard. The next thing policy-makers say is that you don't deserve the vote. They are not looking at students like you, who make up the majority of the students. They are comfortably generalizing about all eighteen-year-olds. All they see is the way people act, but they don't realize there are reasons for this action."

She speaks about why so few black people have become actively involved in the war-protest movement, even though so many black soldiers have been sent to fight and to be killed. Her eyes are fixed. She sits straight up, with her hands folded together, and says each word very distinctly.

"Black people do not see this as their thing. They see it as a middle-class problem, when it really affects all people. But black people have so many here-and-now problems—they do not see that much of the money to solve their problems is tied up in the war. It's not a philosophical thing to them. It's a white man's thing.

"The same is true of Earth Day, that nationwide demonstration supporting clean air and water. They don't see what people are getting so upset about. They see white people going enthusiastically from one issue to another. From the war to Earth Day, still by-passing equal rights. One eighty-five-year-old lady summed the whole feeling up in one statement: 'Polluted water, pol-

luted air. I'm not going to get caught up in that. What
we need a campaign in America about is polluted
hearts. That's what's worrying black people.' "

And she tells them her view on the narcotics problem that everyone is so concerned with these days.
Heroin, she says, has always been a problem in the
black community. In the mid-1950's there was an epi-
demic of heroin addiction in Harlem that killed many
more people than are dying today because of it. But
they were black people, and the problems of crime that
always go along with drug use were black problems,
and no one really cared to solve them. But in the
1970's, heroin is a white problem, too. And congressmen
and politicians, who are also parents, have become
very much concerned about it.

"I've seen the narcotics problem. I've lived it. I have
wallowed in it. It's only now, when the majority is en-
gulfed in this social ill, that anything is being done
about it. I'll tell you what this kind of behavior is, and
I don't think I am incorrect in saying it. It is racism,
whether you want to agree with that evaluation or not."

Other subjects come up too—school busing, the
anger of poor people at the slow rate of improvement in
their lives, women's rights, honest politics.

The session comes to a close. The students thank the
congresswoman for seeing them, and she tells them she
enjoyed talking to them. They were scheduled to stay
half an hour. Their visit lasted an hour and a half. And
now come the telephone calls from New York.

One asks for an endorsement for a congressional candidate running in the Bronx. Representative Chisholm
gives it. The next is not so easy. It is from Mac Holder.

The coming Sunday has been planned as Shirley
Chisholm Day in Brooklyn, with a parade and speeches
and a big dinner at a hotel at the end of the day. The
sponsors are a committee of citizens, with the pastor
of Shirley Chisholm's church serving as chairman. She
has been looking forward to it.

Mac Holder now tells her that the committee, especially the minister, has been asking for money for the
day's events from many people, including Shirley Chisholm's friends in Congress. She is angry and embar-
rassed and makes a decision on the spot. She will with-
draw her name from the day's activities; she says she
will have no part of it. She has not given permission to
collect money from her friends, especially her fellow
congressmen, and she will send them letters of apology.
When this is finished, Shirley Chisholm eats a leisurely
lunch in the House dining room, and then finds an un-
expected addition to her schedule. She had planned to
stay in her office and attend to routine business matters.
But students have invaded Washington as part of the
war protest. The group from Drew had an appointment,
but there are thousands of others who want to see her.
It is impossible to bring them to her. So she goes to
them.

She goes over to the Capitol building a short distance
away and there talks to the students from the steps.
Basically, she tells them the same things she told the
students from Drew, and they are glad to hear it.

She returns to her office and continues to read her
mail and reports. By now it is late afternoon, and she
will soon return to her Washington apartment, fix
herself a light supper, and settle down to more reading.

Some of this reading she will do because she has to, but she always sets some time aside to read the things she enjoys, from classics to books on music, and especially books about the American scene and the role of black people in it. This night will be no exception.

Brooklyn

If Washington can have its quiet, more routine days, Brooklyn never does.

This is a dismal morning, May 8, 1970. The rain keeps trying to fall, and sometimes succeeds. But Shirley, as Representative Chisholm is known in this part of town, rushes into her district office at 587 Eastern Parkway shortly after seven o'clock and provides a sunny hello to the already packed waiting room. The visitors return her greeting. But really they are not visitors. These are the people who put her in Congress, and for them she provides a very special service. Most congressmen have offices in their home districts with a part-time assistant to handle what comes up. Shirley has set up a full-time office for the complaints and problems of her community. There is a staff of three, headed by Mac Holder, and each person is given special care. An average of 150 people a month ask for help.

Every telephone call, every letter, every visit, is listed in a big blue canvas ledger with notations in the margins. Shirley makes notes for Mac Holder, and he makes them for her. No case is lost track of. They are varied—a welfare check hasn't come, the garbage needs collecting, a landlord hasn't fixed a water-faucet break, a mother wants her son's dishonorable discharge from

the Army reinvestigated. Some can be solved by a
phone call or two to the right people. Others require
more work. Community residents can come into the
office anytime, Monday through Thursday, with no
appointment at all, and someone will be there to help.

But sometimes—because the problem is very com-
plicated, or because it is very bothersome, or because
it is a matter that the congresswoman is especially interested in, or just because a person may want to sit
down and see her face to face—appointments are made
on Friday and even on Saturday, for the people to
talk to Shirley.

They come to the office on Eastern Parkway, a
broad tree-lined boulevard with private homes and
six-story apartment buildings, once one of the most
prestigious addresses in Brooklyn. It is a reconverted
doctor's office on the ground floor of a three-story house.
There is a large reception area, lined with chairs and
decorated with posters, one of which says *Free All
Political Prisoners.* Three small staff offices used to be
examining rooms for patients. The door at the end of
the short corridor belongs to Shirley's office. It is old-
looking, but not decaying, very dark with wood-
paneled walls. There is a big desk and high-backed
chair, a flag of the United States, wall shelves that
house a few books, many stacks of papers, and a port-
able television. There is a heavy wooden table, also
stacked with file folders and papers. Under that is a
box of Christmas decorations. A door with a torn screen
leads out to a small garden.

This morning, Shirley whizzes past all of this, look-

ing quite happy. Just last night, she had been admitted
into the Brooklyn Hall of Fame, an honor she was
happy and proud to accept. But this leftover glow cannot interfere with the work that has to be done, and
there is plenty of it. She is already behind schedule.
She sits down, has a cup of tea, thumbs through her
mail and a ledger book that has been set out for her,
and then calls for the first constituent.

A young man comes in. He has been working on a
voter-registration drive in the community and wants
to give his progress report. It is a brief meeting—less
than fifteen minutes—and he leaves. A few minutes
pass, and then in marches the next group. This is a
delegation of teen-agers from Saint Gregory's Church
School, accompanied by a nun. The youngsters, quietly
giggling as they explain their case, are trying to get
money to set up a community center where they can
go to play and socialize. There is no such facility in
their neighborhood, and they have come to the congresswoman for help. Shirley's district has been re-
drawn for the 1970 election, and, as it turns out, Saint
Gregory's will not be included in it. But she will help
anyway. She is only one person in Congress, she tells
the youngsters, but she will do what she can. The meeting is broken up by a knock on the door.

It is Conrad, who has just come from home with important news. The Liberal party has agreed to endorse
Shirley for re-election. If she wants her name to appear
on the June primary ballot, she will have to go to the
party's headquarters in downtown Brooklyn and sign
papers accepting the endorsement.

She thanks the students for coming, grabs her hand-bag, and rushes out of the office with Conrad and one of her aides.

"I'll be right back," she yells to the people waiting in the reception room. "Don't go away."

They nod that they understand.

Outside, she plops into the backseat of the waiting car. Quickly, but not dangerously, Conrad steers it through the crowded streets of Brooklyn. He has had years of experience in getting her from one appointment to another. When he is stopped by traffic lights, people in other cars recognize Shirley and wave to her. In twenty minutes, the party arrives at the office building on Court Street. It is raining now. Shirley stays in the car while her aide goes to the trunk for a blue-and-white striped umbrella belonging to an airline. Under its protection, she sweeps into the building. The elevator man recognizes her, and asks her aide in Spanish, "Is that the congresswoman?" Shirley answers him herself. In Spanish.

"Comes in so handy, this Spanish," she remarks more to herself than anyone in particular, as she walks into the elevator.

The signing takes only a few minutes, and then there is a rush back to the office to continue meeting with the people. The schedule is all off by now.

The next visitor is a city commissioner who has come to talk about political matters—suggestions for appoint-ments for jobs. Again a short session, and he leaves with a smile.

Next are representatives of the Crown Heights Com-munity Council. They want to discuss housing prob-

lems in their area and their efforts to create a more
peaceful relationship between black and white residents in the community.

Then there is a delegation from School District Six
in Manhattan. They are trying to get an acting principal
in one of their schools appointed to permanent status.
This is not easy to do in New York, where principals
can only be chosen from a list of those who have passed
a test for the job. New York is the only city in the state
that has a Board of Examiners, which requires this test.
Because the city's public-school system has a very small
percentage of minority-group principals, the test has
been called discriminatory in its effect. So a federal
court judge would finally rule in 1971, striking down the
test.

The situation had become critical when black people
began demanding black principals for schools in their
neighborhoods. But at this time, in 1970, there were
none on the list. And every person on the list would
have to turn the job down before District Six could
appoint someone else—no matter how well qualified.
It was an unlikely event when there were some two
hundred people waiting for a principal's post listed.

The problem came up again and again. It did several
times in Harlem. It exploded in the Ocean Hill-Brownsville district in Brooklyn, and now Manhattan was
affected again. Congresswoman Chisholm knows the
frustrations of this situation well, and she assures the
delegation that she will work on it, meaning that she
will make calls to people who can help.

When they leave, Shirley sits back and sighs. The
day has really just begun. She has promised Conrad

she would not stay in the office past 1:00 P.M. A bit after that hour, he picks her up, and she goes the few blocks to her home for a brief lunch and an afternoon nap.

She wakes up, dresses, and hurries to Manhattan to tape a television show that will be seen the following Monday. This is at six o'clock. At seven she is due back in Brooklyn to speak before the Lindsay Park Tenants' Council. After almost an hour there, she goes home again to change into formal clothes, and then it's back to Harlem for a dance given by the Federation of Negro Civil Service Organizations. A short speech, some dancing, then home, and to bed. Tomorrow, there will be a luncheon in New Jersey and more evening activities before Shirley Chisholm has to get back to Washington, which is almost calm, if you compare it with Brooklyn.

Chapter 8

The Durable Maverick

The people dig Shirley Chisholm. The politicians do not. Where does that leave her as a future force in this country?

"I never said I was in politics to stay," she answers, "I know it can end at any moment."

But there are real questions about the significance of Shirley Chisholm, the skinny little schoolteacher with the fearless mouth who turned out to be a political dynamo. The biggest one: Are the professional politicians just letting her have her way now, and planning to destroy her—figuratively—in the future? *Can* a person of such independence have any real power? What if, for example, her amendment for change of committee had been turned down? It was not, but why wasn't it? These are questions that she, too, must surely think about.

In the meantime, she continues to go her own way, doing and saying what she believes in. But it is not always easy to be a maverick.

In the New York mayoral election of 1969, the Democratic party nominated Mario Procaccino, who campaigned on a law-and-order platform. In the Republican party primary, the voters by-passed Mayor John V. Lindsay. But he was running for re-election as the Liberal party candidate and on an Independent party line. As the Democratic state party chairman, Shirley Chisholm was expected to support the party's candidate. Although her post would be in danger and her friends advised against it, she gave her backing to Lindsay.

There was another celebrated occasion when Shirley Chisholm went her own way despite the fact that it would probably have been much easier not to. That was in April, 1970.

The scene was Grossinger's, a luxury resort in New York State's Catskill Mountains. Each spring and summer and on holidays throughout the year, vacationers flock to its indoor pool and nightclubs for rest and relaxation. Shirley Chisholm did not go for any such things as these. The New York State Democratic Committee, of which she was still chairman, was meeting to designate its choice of a candidate to run against Governor Nelson A. Rockefeller, who had then been in office twelve years. She was not there alone. With her was a community delegation, mostly women, who had come to watch politics in action.

She did not go as a nonpartisan leader. It was no secret that her choice was Howard J. Samuels, an upstate businessman distinguished by a fine head of wavy silver hair. He had been a friend to the black community as chief of the Small Business Administration during the Johnson presidency. He was later to be well known to New Yorkers as head of the city's Off Track Betting Corporation. Most of the delegates were supporting Arthur J. Goldberg, former secretary of labor, associate justice of the Supreme Court, and United States representative to the United Nations.

There was much controversy about the Goldberg candidacy. Goldberg had been saying all along that he would not run, although most political experts believed he really planned to. His critics said he was just unwilling to go out and campaign among the people. They said he wanted to be "crowned governor of New York State."

A difficult fight was expected to develop around his candidacy, but it didn't. An entirely different issue came up. All along it had been understood that a black state senator, Basil A. Paterson, would be designated to run for lieutenant governor. But once everyone had arrived at Grossinger's, there began to be whispers of "Goldberg is going to dump Basil."

Shirley Chisholm was furious. Her community contingent from Brooklyn was furious. One young activist went to the stage and tried to tell the delegates that if they took Basil Paterson off the ticket, it would be a slap at the black community. The delegates did not listen.

So Shirley Chisholm rose and went to the microphone, very composed, very quiet. She was wearing a white dress and looked angelic, more like a schoolteacher than a political power.

"Please," she said to the auditorium full of delegates sitting and standing, talking and shouting. Very few were listening. But they looked up and saw her, and after a bit they quieted down.

"I'm not planning to make a speech," she said, and ten minutes later, when she was still standing there talking, she said it again. "But how could you do this? You ought to be ashamed of yourselves. You say you want change, but you don't want change." The words shot out one at a time like bullets from a gun. "Just look at you. You have a chance to support a worthy candidate, State Senator Basil A. Paterson, and look at what you're doing."

"Get off that stage!" screamed a woman in the Nassau County delegation.

"You come up here and get me off!" was Shirley Chisholm's reply. And she continued. She spoke of "wheeling and dealing" and "footsy and games." Her face became more intense, and she was more angry. She called for a walkout of all black delegates to meet for a "black caucus."

"Will those with courage and guts—and it takes guts in a rigged convention—leave this floor and meet with us?" she demanded. By then, the general meeting was disrupted.

The party leaders told her that they could not run Senator Paterson. There would be three Jewish candidates on the ticket, and they could not add a black man, a member of another minority, to that. Their concern reflected one of the fixed ideas of politics, called balancing the ticket. This involves trying to represent as many different ethnic backgrounds as possible to

appeal to all voters. Shirley Chisholm's answer to them
was simple: "If that's what you're so worried about, take
one of the Jewish candidates off the ticket."

"They just made me furious," she said later. "Friends
of mine who saw the television broadcast of that speech
said that I looked so angry that they thought I was
going to have a heart attack right there on the stage
and fall dead."

But it all paid off. After the deal had been exposed
to everyone, it could no longer be carried off. The Democratic party endorsed Basil Paterson for lieutenant
governor. But it did not give its support to Howard
Samuels as the candidate for governor.

Shirley Chisholm admired this man. Although the
party had rejected him, there was still the primary
election in June, when the voters would choose the candidates. She set up a Brooklyn campaign office for
Samuels as part of her own, right around the corner
from her Bedford-Stuyvesant district office. She spoke
on his behalf and sought opportunities to increase support for him.

There was, for instance, one formal evening that May
at New York's famous old Waldorf Astoria Hotel, a
favored setting for important political affairs. This
gathering was the Frederick Douglass Memorial Awards
dinner of the New York Urban League. Frederick Douglass was the brilliant abolitionist speaker and writer
who had escaped from slavery in Maryland in 1838
and made his way to Rochester, New York, where he
founded and edited the newspaper *North Star*. He re-
cruited black troops in the Civil War, and was later
the United States minister to Haiti. The New York Ur-

ban League is the largest chapter of the National
Urban League, which has been working for years to
find better jobs and better housing for black people
and to fight against discrimination in the North as well
as the South.

The dinner was a grand occasion. All the national
black figures were there. White leaders of industry and
civic organizations were there. All the candidates running for governor were there—except one: Howard J.
Samuels. Shirley Chisholm was supposed to be there.
She was a co-chairman of the evening and had helped
plan it. But it had been a busy day in Washington, and
she would have to stay late to vote on some important
bills. No one was certain whether she would be able to
make it.

She was not there by the time the guests had sat
down to their banquet dinner at round tables for ten
that filled the ballroom floor. The candidates for governor were among them. Up on the stage were seats for
the co-chairmen. Two were empty—Shirley Chisholm's
and one beside hers. The guests had surrendered their
tickets to the waiters, entitling them to be served their
$100-a-plate meal. Still no Shirley Chisholm. The guests
were eating their main course when in swept a figure in
a blue brocade dress with a little jacket. It was unmis-
takably Shirley Chisholm, and there was someone with
her, a man with wavy silver hair. She whispered something to him and began her walk across the huge ballroom floor, packed with tables full of diners. He followed right behind her, and no one could fail to recognize Howard Samuels. She walked up onto the stage

and took her seat. He followed. Shirley Chisholm had engineered a dramatic campaign endorsement without ever saying a word.

The professional politicians have learned that she knows how to wield power in many ways. Incidents such as the battle of Grossinger's and the fight over her committee assignment in Congress have convinced them that she is a maverick with staying power. Nowadays, almost every Democrat running for office would like to have her endorsement. Those who think they have a good enough cause or political record would like her to campaign for them. It is a far cry from the days when she bucked the regulars and won her congressional seat. In her re-election campaign in 1970 she took nothing for granted, once again going to the voters and discussing the issues. Her opponents, the Republican John Coleman and a Conservative candidate, together polled only a bit better than 7,000 votes. Shirley Chisholm received more than four votes for every one of theirs. Her total was 31,308.

Nowadays, also, when jobs are given out in New York City and New York State, Shirley Chisholm has something to say about them. Her name keeps popping up for other jobs, higher positions—Shirley Chisholm for senator, Shirley Chisholm for president. She smiles and takes this as recognition that she is doing a good job.

"I'm trying to show young people, black people, poor people, by my every action and word, not to give up. This government belongs to them. They should know it and take the responsibility for running it. Politics has a negative sound to it, but we have to work to take it out of the local clubhouses and give it to the people. This is the role I have to play.

"It's a hard job. I'm older now and can't run the way I could when I started this fifteen years ago. But I'm going to keep going, until I just can't anymore."

Acknowledgments

The author wishes to thank especially Charlayne Hunter, chief of the Harlem bureau of *The New York Times,* and Richard Bruner, author of *Black Politicians,* a young-adult book published in June 1971, by the David McKay Co., Inc.

INDEX

NANCY HICKS is a reporter for *The New York Times*. Before that, she was with *The New York Post,* where she received the New York Urban League's 1967 Russwurm Award for excellence in journalism. Mrs. Hicks is a graduate of Long Island University. She lives in New York with her husband, Daniel, and their recently born son, David.